To Frank

Get well soon!

Love

Martin & Phyll

DEEDS OF VALOUR
A Victorian Military and Naval History Trilogy

JAMES W BANCROFT

© James W Bancroft MCMXCIX

Published in 1994 by
The House of Heroes
280 Liverpool Road
Eccles M30 ORZ

Telephone: 061 707 6455

ISBN: 0 9524014 0 1

All Rights Reserved. No part of this publication may be reproduced without written permission from the author and his contributors.

Titles and Cover Design by
James W Bancroft

Printed by
E. & E. Plumridge Ltd., Linton, Cambridge

CONTENTS

THE CHRONOLOGY OF VICTORIAN VCs
With An Analysis of VC Citations, 1857-1905   1

A RORKE'S DRIFT MAN
The Life of Sergeant Henry Gallagher, 24th Regiment   41

VICTORIAN NAVAL BATTLES AND DISASTERS
A Selection of Eyewitness Accounts

The Bombardment of Acre, 1840   64

Rangoon: Storming the Golden Pagoda, 1852   72

The Wreck of the Troopship *Birkenhead*, 1852   81

The Baltic Fleet, 1854   91

The Burning of the Transport *Sarah Sands*, 1857   99

The First Ironclad Fight: The *Merrimac* and the *Monitor*, 1862   107

The Burning of the Battleship *Bombay*, 1864   116

The Bombardment of Alexandria, 1882   126

Disaster on HMS *Calliope*, 1889; and on HMS *Victoria*, 1893   135

PREFACE

I compiled the Chronology of Victorian VCs while undertaking a study of all the citations published in the *London Gazette* from 1857 to 1905, and I trust my analysis will be of interest to students of the Victoria Cross and military history in general.

I am indebted to George Wentworth for allowing me access to his excellent collection of photographs and official documents concerning Sergeant Henry Gallagher, 24th Regiment, who was a defender of Rorke's Drift. I am also grateful to Major Edward Lane, RE (retired), who, as Henry Gallagher's oldest surviving grandchild, was kind enough to share his reminiscences and offer guidance.

The eyewitness accounts of Victorian naval battles and disasters were originally published in the *Royal Magazine* between 1905 and 1911. As far as I am aware they have not appeared in any bibliography, and thus will provide an interesting source of information for Naval enthusiasts.

James W Bancroft, 1994.

THE CHRONOLOGY OF VICTORIAN VCs

'In those days there was no Victoria Cross, yet soldiers did not do lesser deeds because there was no bronze recognition of their valour. They took up fighting as their life's trade – once a soldier always a soldier was a pretty general rule; and there was no chance for a young man who had scarcely learnt to march talking about having a claim on his country because he had served it.'

Private John Howton, 50th Regiment, a veteran of the 1st Sikh War, 1845/46

CRIMEAN WAR

21 June 1854   Bomarsund, Baltic Sea
Mate Charles D Lucas, Royal Navy

8-12 August   Wardo Island, Baltic Sea
Lieutenant John Bythesea, Royal Navy
Stoker William Johnstone, Royal Navy

20 September   River Alma
a) Sergeant Luke O'Connor, 23rd Regiment
   Captain Edward D Bell, 23rd Regiment
b) Captain Robert J Lindsay, Scots Fusilier Guards
c) Lieutenant John S Knox, Scots Fusilier Guards
   Sergeant James McKechnie, Scots Fusilier Guards
   Private William Reynolds, Scots Fusilier Guards
d) Sergeant John Park, 77th Regiment
   a) also 8 September 1855 – The Redan, Sebastopol
   b) also 5 November 1854 – Inkerman
   c) also 18 June 1855 – The Redan, Sebastopol – with the Rifle Brigade
   d) also 5 November 1854 – Inkerman; 19 April 1855 – Sebastopol; 18 June and 8 September 1855 – The Redan, Sebastopol

17 October   Sebastopol
Colonel Collingwood Dickson, Royal Artillery

18 October   Sebastopol
Private Thomas Grady, 4th Regiment
also 22 November 1854 – Sebastopol

25 October   Balaclava
Sergeant-Major John Grieve, 2nd Royal Dragoons
Sergeant Henry Ramage, 2nd Royal Dragoons
Surgeon James Mouat, 6th Dragoons
Private Samuel Parkes, 4th Light Dragoons
Lieutenant Alexander R Dunn, 11th Hussars
Corporal Joseph Malone, 13th Light Dragoons
Troop-Sergeant-Major John Berryman, 17th Lancers
Quartermaster-Sergeant John Farrell, 17th Lancers
Sergeant-Major Charles Wooden, 17th Lancers

26 October   Little Inkerman
Private William Stanlack, Coldstream Guards
Sergeant-Major Ambrose Maddan, 41st Regiment
Lieutenant John A Conolly, 49th Regiment

28 October   Sebastopol
Brevet-Major Gerald L Goodlake, Coldstream Guards

30 October Sebastopol
Corporal James Owens, 49th Regiment

5 November Inkerman
a) Captain William Peel, Naval Brigade
b) Lieutenant William N W Hewett, Naval Brigade
c) Midshipman Edward St J Daniel, Naval Bridge
Seaman Thomas Reeves, Naval Brigade
Seaman James Gorman, Naval Brigade
Seaman Mark Scholefield, Naval Brigade
Corporal John Prettyjohn, Royal Marine Light Infantry
Major Frederick Miller, Royal Artillery
Sergeant-Major Andrew Henry, Royal Artillery
Colonel, The Hon. Henry H M Percy, Grenadier Guards
Captain, Sir Charles Russell, Grenadier Guards
Private Anthony Palmer, Grenadier Guards
Lieutenant Mark Walker, 30th Regiment
Captain Hugh Rowlands, 41st Regiment
Private John McDermond, 47th Regiment
Sergeant George Walters, 49th Regiment
Private Thomas Beach, 55th Regiment
d) Private John Byrne, 68th Regiment
Lieutenant, The Hon. Henry H Clifford, Rifle Brigade
a) also 18 October 1854 – Sebastopol and 18 June 1855 – The Redan, Sebastopol
b) also 26 October 1854 – Little Inkerman
c) also 18 October 1854 – Sebastopol and 18 June 1855 – The Redan, Sebastopol
d) also 11 May 1855 – Sebastopol

10 November Sebastopol
Private Francis Wheatley, Rifle Brigade

20 November Rifle Pits, Sebastopol
Lieutenant Wilbraham O Lennox, Royal Engineers
Captain William J M Cunninghame, Rifle Brigade
Captain Claud T Bourchier, Rifle Brigade

19 December White Horse Revine, Sebastopol
Private William Norman, 7th Regiment

14 February 1855 Sebastopol
Corporal William J Lendrim, Royal Engineers
also 11 April and 20 April 1855 – Sebastopol

22 March Sebastopol
Private Alexander Wright, 77th Regiment
also 19 April and 30 August 1855 – Sebastopol

29 March   Sebastopol
Private William Coffey, 34th Regiment

10 April   Sebastopol
Botswains-Mate John Sullivan, Naval Bridge

13 April   Sebastopol
Private Samuel Evans, 19th Regiment

17 April   Sebastopol
Captain Matthew C Dixon, Royal Artillery

19 April   Sebastopol
Colour-Sergeant Henry McDonald, Royal Engineers

22 April   Sebastopol
Private Joseph Bradshaw, Rifle Brigade
Private Robert Humpston, Rifle Brigade
* Private Roderick McGregor, Rifle Brigade
* also July 1855 – Sebastopol

11 May   Sebastopol
Captain Thomas de C Hamilton, 68th Regiment

29 May   Sea of Azov
Lieutenant Cecil W Buckley, Royal Navy
Lieutenant Hugh T Burgoyne, Royal Navy
Gunner John Robarts, Royal Navy

3 June   Sea of Azov
Botswain Henry Cooper, Royal Navy

6 June   Sebastopol
Sergeant George Symons, Royal Artillery

7 June   The Quarries, Sebastopol
Bombardier Thomas Wilkinson, Royal Marine Artillery
Captain Henry M Jones, 7th Regiment
* Captain Frederick C Elton, 55th Regiment
* also 22 March and 4 August 1855 – Sebastopol

10 June   Sebastopol
Private John Lyons, 19th Regiment

16 June   Sebastopol
Private Joseph Prosser, 1st Regiment
also 11 August 1855 – Sebastopol

18 June   The Redan, Sebastopol
Commander Henry J Raby, Naval Brigade
Captain of the Forecastle John Taylor, Naval Brigade
Botswains-Mate Henry Curtis, Naval Brigade

a) Gunner Thomas Arthur, Royal Artillery
   Captain Howard C Elphinstone, Royal Engineers
   Lieutenant Gerald Graham, Royal Engineers
   Colour-Sergeant Peter Leitch, Royal Engineers
   Sapper John Perie, Royal Engineers
   Lieutenant William Hope, 7th Regiment
b) Private Matthew Hughes, 7th Regiment
   Corporal Philip Smith, 17th Regiment
c) Captain Thomas Esmonde, 18th Regiment
   Private John J Sims, 34th Regiment
d) Sergeant William McWheeney, 44th Regiment
e) Colour-Sergeant George Gardiner, 57th Regiment
f) Private John Alexander, 90th Regiment
   a) also 7 June 1855 – The Quarries, Sebastopol
   b) also 7 June 1855 – The Quarries, Sebastopol
   c) also 20 June 1855 – Sebastopol
   d) also 20 October and 5 December 1854 – Sebastopol
   e) also 22 March 1855 – Sebastopol
   f) also 6 September 1855 – Sebastopol
   see 20 September 1854 – The River Alma
   see 5 November 1854 – Inkerman

23 June Sebastopol
Private Charles McCorrie, 57th Regiment

3 July Genitchi, Sea of Azov
Seaman Joseph Trewavas, Royal Navy

13 July Viborg, Baltic Sea
Captain of the Maintop George H Ingouville, Royal Navy
Lieutenant George D Dowell, Royal Navy

13 July Sebastopol
Botswain John Shephard, Naval Brigade

30 August Sebastopol
Sergeant John Coleman, 97th Regiment

31 August Marionpol
Botswain Joseph Kellaway, Royal Navy

2 September Sebastopol
Sergeant Alfred Ablett, Grenadier Guards

6 September The Redan, Sebastopol
Sergeant James Craig, Scots Fusilier Guards

8 September The Redan, Sebastopol
Captain Gronow Davis, Royal Artillery
Bombardier Daniel Cambridge, Royal Artillery

a) Corporal John Ross, Royal Engineers
Lieutenant-Colonel Frederick F Maude, 3rd Regiment
Private John Connors, 3rd Regiment
Assistant-Surgeon William T E Hale, 7th Regiment
Assistant-Surgeon Henry T Sylvester, 23rd Regiment
Corporal Robert Shields, 23rd Regiment
Ensign Andrew Moynihan, 90th Regiment
Captain Charles H Lumley, 97th Regiment
*a) also 21 July and 23 August 1855 – Sebastopol
see 20 September 1854 – The River Alma*

September Sebastopol
Private George Strong, Coldstream Guards

17 to 29 September Genitchi, Sea of Azov
Commander George F Day, Royal Navy

29 September Kars
Lieutenant Christopher C Teesdale, Royal Artillery

11 October Sivash, Sea of Azov
Commander John E Commerell, Royal Navy
Quartermaster William T Rickard, Royal Navy

PERSIA

9 December 1856 Bushire
Captain John A Wood, 20th Bombay Native Infantry

8 February 1857 Khoosh-ab
Lieutenant and Adjutant Arthur T Moore, 3rd Bombay Light Cavalry
Lieutenant John G Malcolmson, 3rd Bombay Light Cavalry

INDIAN MUTINY

11 May 1857 Delhi Magazine
Conductor John Buckley, Army Ordnance Department
Conductor George Forrest, Bengal Veterans Establishment
Conductor William Raynor, Bengal Veterans Establishment

4 June Benares
Private John Kirk, 10th Regiment
Sergeant-Major Peter Gill, 15th Ludhiana Sikhs
Sergeant-Major Matthew Rosamond, 37th Bengal Native Infantry

8 June Budle-ke-Serai, near Delhi
Lieutenant Alfred S Jones, 9th Lancers
a) Sergeant Henry Hartigan, 9th Lancers
b) Colour-Sergeant Cornelius Coghlan, 75th Highlanders
  a) also 10 October 1857 – Agra
  b) also 18 July 1857 – Subjee Mundee, Delhi

12 June Flagstaff Picquet, Delhi
Lieutenant Thomas Cadell, 2nd European Bengal Fusiliers

19 June Delhi
Private Thomas Hancock, 9th Lancers
Private John Purcell, 9th Lancers
Private Samuel Turner, 60th Rifles

23 June Delhi
Colour-Sergeant Stephen Garvin, 60th Rifles
Private John McGovern, 1st European Bengal Fusiliers

30 June Lucknow
Private William Oxenham, 32nd Regiment

30 June Chinhut, near Delhi
Lieutenant William G Cubitt, 13th Bengal Native Infantry

1 July Indore Presidency
Colonel James Travers, 2nd Bengal Native Infantry

7 July Jhelum
Gunner William Connolly, Bengal Artillery

9 July Delhi
Lieutenant-Colonel Henry Tombs, Bengal Artillery
Lieutenant James Hills, Bengal Artillery
Private James Thompson, 60th Rifles

10 July Kolapore
Lieutenant William A Kerr, 24th Bombay Native Infantry

16 July Cawnpore
Lieutenant Henry M Havelock, 10th Regiment

18 July Subjee-Mundee, Delhi
Lieutenant Richard Wadeson, 75th Highlanders

29 July Onao
Lieutenant Andrew C Bogle, 78th Highlanders

30 July Arrah
* Private Denis Dempsey, 10th Regiment
Mr William F McDonell, Bengal Civil Service
Mr Ross L Mangles, Bengal Civil Service
  * also 12 August 1857 – Ingdispore, and 14 March 1858 – Lucknow

12 August   Boorzeke-Chowkee
Lieutenant Joseph P H Crowe, 78th Highlanders

12 August   Neemuch
Captain James Blair, 2nd Bombay Light Cavalry
also 23 October 1857 – Jeerum

15 & 18 August   Khurkowdah, near Rhotuck
Major Charles J S Gough, 5th Bengal European Cavalry
also 27 January 1858 – Shumshabad, and 23 February 1858 – Meangunge

21 August   Lucknow Residency
Captain Henry G Browne, 32nd Regiment

10 September   Delhi
Private John Divane, 60th Rifles

11 September   Koodsia Bagh, Delhi
Private Patrick Green, 75th Highlanders

13 September   Delhi
Bugler William Sutton, 60th Rifles
also 2 August 1857 – Delhi

14 September   Relief of Delhi
Lieutenant Duncan C Home, Bengal Engineers
Lieutenant Philip Salkeld, Bengal Engineers
Sapper-Sergeant John Smith, Bengal Sappers & Miners
Lance-Corporal Henry Smith, 52nd Regiment
Bugler Robert Hawthorne, 52nd Regiment
Colour-Sergeant George Waller, 60th Rifles
* Surgeon Herbert T Reade, 61st Regiment
Sergeant James McGuire, 1st European Bengal Fusiliers
Drummer Miles Ryan, 1st European Bengal Fusiliers
Captain Robert H Shebbeare, 60th Bengal Native Infantry
* also 16 September 1857 – Delhi

16 September   Delhi Magazine
Lieutenant Edward T Thackeray, Royal Engineers
Captain George A Renny, Bengal Artillery

18 September   Siege of Delhi
Lieutenant Alfred S Heathcote, 60th Rifles
Ensign Everard A L Phillips, 11th Bengal Native Infantry

21 September   Mungulwar
Sergeant Patrick Mahoney, 1st European Madras Fusiliers

24 September   Alum Bagh, Lucknow
Private Robert Grant, 5th Regiment

25 September Siege of Lucknow
* Sergeant-Major George Lambert, 84th Regiment
  Lance-Corporal Abraham Boulger, 84th Regiment
  Private Joel Holmes, 84th Regiment
  * *also 29 July 1857 – Onao, and 16 August 1857 – Bithoor*

25 September Relief of Lucknow
  Captain Francis C Maude, Royal Artillery
  Captain William Olpherts, Royal Artillery
  Lieutenant Herbert T McPherson, 78th Highlanders
a) Private Henry Ward, 78th Highlanders
  Surgeon Joseph Jee, 78th Highlanders
  Assistant-Surgeon Valentine M McMaster, 78th Highlanders
b) Lieutenant William Rennie, 90th Regiment
  a) also 26 September 1857 – Lucknow
  b) also 21 September 1857 – Lucknow

26 September Relief of Lucknow
  Private Peter McManus, 5th Regiment
* Lieutenant Samuel H Lawrence, 32nd Regiment
  Colour-Sergeant Stewart McPherson, 78th Highlanders
  Private James Hollowell, 78th Highlanders
  Surgeon Anthony D Home, 90th Regiment
  Assistant-Surgeon William Bradshaw, 90th Regiment
  Private John Ryan, 1st European Madras Fusiliers
  Private Thomas Duffy, 1st European Madras Fusiliers
  * *also 7 July 1857 – Lucknow*

27 September Lucknow
  Bombardier Jacob Thomas, Bengal Artillery
  Private William Dowling, 32nd Regiment

28 September Bolundshahur
  Lieutenant Robert Blair, Dragoon Guards
  Lance-Corporal Robert Kells, 9th Lancers
  Private Patrick Donohoe, 9th Lancers
  Private James R Roberts, 9th Lancers
  Sergeant Bernard Diamond, Bengal Artillery
  Gunner Richard Fitzgerald, Bengal Artillery
  see 16 November 1857 – 2nd Relief of Lucknow

2 October Chota Bahar
  Sergeant Denis Dynon, 53rd Regiment
* Lieutenant John C C Daunt, 11th Bengal Native Infantry
  * *also 2 November 1857 – Lucknow*

2 October Siege of Lucknow
  Private Patrick McHale, 5th Regiment
  also 22 December 1857 – Lucknow

6 October   Siege of Lucknow
Lance-Corporal John Sinnott, 84th Regiment

10 October   Agra
Private John Freeman, 9th Lancers

28 October   Futtehpore
Conductor James Miller, Army Ordnance Department (Bengal)

9 November   Siege of Lucknow
Mr Thomas H Kavanagh, Bengal Civil Service

12 November   Alum Bagh, Lucknow
Lieutenant Hugh H Gough, 1st Bengal Cavalry
also 25 February 1858 – Jellalabad

14 November   Dilkusha Park, Lucknow
Lieutenant John Watson, 1st Punjab Cavalry
Captain Dighton M Probyn, 2nd Punjab Cavalry

16 November   Narnaul
Lieutenant Francis D M Brown, 1st European Bengal Fusiliers

16 November   2nd Relief of Lucknow
Lieutenant Nowell Salmon, Naval Bridge
Lieutenant Thomas J Young, Naval Bridge
Botswains-Mate John Harrison, Naval Bridge
Able Seaman William Hall, Naval Bridge
Lieutenant Alfred K Ffrench, 53rd Regiment
Private Charles Irwin, 53rd Regiment
Private James Kenny, 53rd Regiment
* Captain Augustus H A Anson, 84th Regiment
Major John C Guise, 90th Regiment
Sergeant Samuel Hill, 90th Regiment
Captain William G D Stewart, 93rd Highlanders
Colour-Sergeant James Munro, 93rd Highlanders
Sergeant John Paton, 93rd Highlanders
Lance-Corporal John Dunlay, 93rd Highlanders
Private Peter Grant, 93rd Highlanders
Private David Mackay, 93rd Highlanders
Private John Smith, 1st European Madras Fusiliers
* *also 28 September 1857 – Bolundshahur*

17 November   2nd Relief of Lucknow
Sergeant-Major Charles C Pye, 53rd Regiment
* Private Patrick Mylott, 84th Regiment
Private Patrick Graham, 90th Regiment
* *and throughout the Siege of Lucknow*

18 November   2nd Relief of Lucknow
Lieutenant Thomas B Hacklett, 23rd Regiment
Private George Monger, 23rd Regiment

14 to 22 November   2nd Relief of Lucknow
Lieutenant Hastings E Harington, Bengal Artillery
Rough Rider Edward Jennings, Bengal Artillery
Gunner Thomas Laughnan, Bengal Artillery
Gunner Hugh McInnes, Bengal Artillery
Gunner James Park, Bengal Artillery

21 November   Mundisore
Lieutenant Henry N D Prendergast, Madras Engineers
also at Ratgurh, and 1 April 1858 – River Betwah, near Jhansi

30 June to 22 November.   Defence of Lucknow.
Lieutenant Robert H M Aitken, 13th Bengal Native Infantry.

28 November   Cawnpore
Drummer Thomas Flinn, 64th Regiment

2 January 1858   Khadagunge
Lieutenant Frederick S Roberts, Royal Artillery

6 January   Rowa
Private Bernard McQuirt, 95th Regiment

27 January   Shumsabad
Troop Sergeant-Major David Spence, 9th Lancers

10 February   Choorpoorah
Lieutenant John A Tytler, 66th Punjabis

23 February   Sultanpore
Lieutenant John J M Innes, Bengal Engineers

1 March   River Goomtee, Lucknow
Lieutenant Frederick R Aikman, 4th Bengal Native Infantry

6 March   Lucknow
Lance Corporal William Goate, 9th Lancers

9 March   Lucknow
Lieutenant Francis E H Farquharson, 42nd Highlanders
Lieutenant Thomas A Butler, 1st European Bengal Fusiliers

11 March   Begum Bagh, Lucknow
Lieutenant William McBean, 93rd Highlanders

11 March   Iron Bridge, Lucknow
Captain Henry Wilmot, Rifle Brigade
Corporal William Nash, Rifle Brigade
Private David Hawkes, Rifle Brigade

13 March   Begum Kotee, Lucknow
Able-Seaman Edward Robinson, Naval Brigade

17 March   Chundairee
Major Richard H Keatinge, Bombay Artillery

19 March   Moosa Bagh, Lucknow
Cornet William G H Bankes, 7th Hussars

19 March   Lucknow
Troop Sergeant-Major David Rush, 9th Lancers
Private Robert Newell, 9th Lancers

30 March   Kotah
Lieutenant Aylmer S Cameron, 72nd Highlanders

1 April   River Betwah, near Jhansi
Lieutenant James Leitch, 14th Hussars
Lieutenant Hugh S Cochrane, 86th Rifles

3 April   Jhansi
Bombardier Joseph Brennan, Royal Artillery
Corporal Michael Sleavon, Royal Engineers
a) Captain Henry E Jerome, 86th Rifles
Private James Byrne, 86th Rifles
b) Private James Pearson, 86th Rifles
c) Private Frederick Whirlpool, 3rd Bombay European Regiment
  a) also 28 May 1858 – *Jumna*
  b) also 23 May 1858 – *Calpee*
  c) also 2 May 1858 – *Lohari*

6 April   Azimghur
Sergeant William Napier, 13th Regiment
Private Patrick Carlin, 13th Regiment

15 April   Azimghur
Private Samuel Morley, Military Train
Private Michael Murphy, Military Train

15 April   Fort Ruiyah
Quartermaster-Sergeant John Simpson, 42nd Highlanders
Lance-Corporal Alexander Thompson, 42nd Highlanders
Private James Davis, 42nd Highlanders
Private Edward Spense, 42nd Highlanders
Captain William F Cafe, 56th Punjabi Rifles

5 May   Bareilly
Colour-Sergeant William Gardner, 42nd Highlanders

6 May   Bareilly
Private Valentine Bambrick, 60th Rifles

23 May   Calpee
Lieutenant Harry H Lyster, 72nd Punjabi Infantry

13 June   Nawab Gunge, Lucknow
Private Same Shaw, Rifle Brigade

16 June   Marar, near Gwalior
Private George Rodgers, 71st Highlanders

17 June   Gwalior
Captain Clement W Heneage, 8th Hussars
Sergeant Joseph Ward, 8th Hussars
Farrier George Hollis, 8th Hussars
Private John Pearson, 8th Hussars

20 June   Gwalior
Lieutenant William F F Waller, 25th Bombay Light Infantry

31 August   Seerporah
Lieutenant-Colonel Samuel J Browne, 46th Bengal Native Infantry

8 September   Beejapore
Troop Sergeant-Major James Champion, 8th Hussars
also 17 June 1858 – Gwalior

27 September   Suhejnee, near Peroo
Volunteer George B Chicken, Naval Bridge
Lieutenant Charles G Baker, Bengal Police Battalion

27 September   Kuthirga
Ensign Patrick Roddy, Bengal Army

8 October   Jamo, near Sandeela
Trumpeter Thomas Monaghan, 2nd Dragoon Guards
Private Charles Anderson, 2nd Dragoon Guards

14 October   Baroun
Lieutenant Hanson C Jarrett, 26th Bengal Native Infantry

19 October   Sindwaho
Lieutenant H Evelyn Wood, 17th Lancers

31 December   River Raptee
Major Charles C Fraser, 7th Hussars

2 January 1859   Kurrereah
Private Henry Addison, 43rd Regiment

15 January   Maylar Ghaut
Private Walter Cook, 42nd Highlanders
Private Duncan Miller, 42nd Highlanders

15 January   Chichumbah
Captain Herbert M Clogstoun, 19th Madras Native Infantry

27 April   Kewanie
Private George Richardson, 34th Regiment

6 October   Fort Beyt, Kattywar
Lieutenant Charles A Goodfellow, Bengal Engineers

CHINA

21 August 1860   Taku Forts
Lieutenant Robert M Rogers, 44th Regiment
Private John McDougall, 44th Regiment
Lieutenant Edmund H Lenon, 67th Regiment
Lieutenant Nathaniel Burslem, 67th Regiment
Ensign John W Chaplin, 67th Regiment
Private Thomas Lane, 67th Regiment
Hospital Apprentice Andrew Fitzgibbon, Indian Medical Department

9 October 1862   Fung Wha
Able-Seaman George Hinckley, Royal Navy

NEW ZEALAND

28 March 1860   Waireka
Leading-Seaman William Odgers, Navy Navy

18 March 1861   Huirangi Bush
Colour-Sergeant John Lucas, 40th Regiment

INDIA

30 October 1863   Crag Picquet, Umbeyla
Lieutenant George V Fosbury, 4th Bengal European Regiment
Lieutenant Henry W Pitcher, 4th Punjab Infantry

NEW ZEALAND

7 September 1863   Cameron Town
Colour-Sergeant Edward McKenna, 65th Regiment
Lance-Corporal John Ryan, 65th Regiment

The Battle of the Alma, 1854

The Battle of Inkerman, 1854

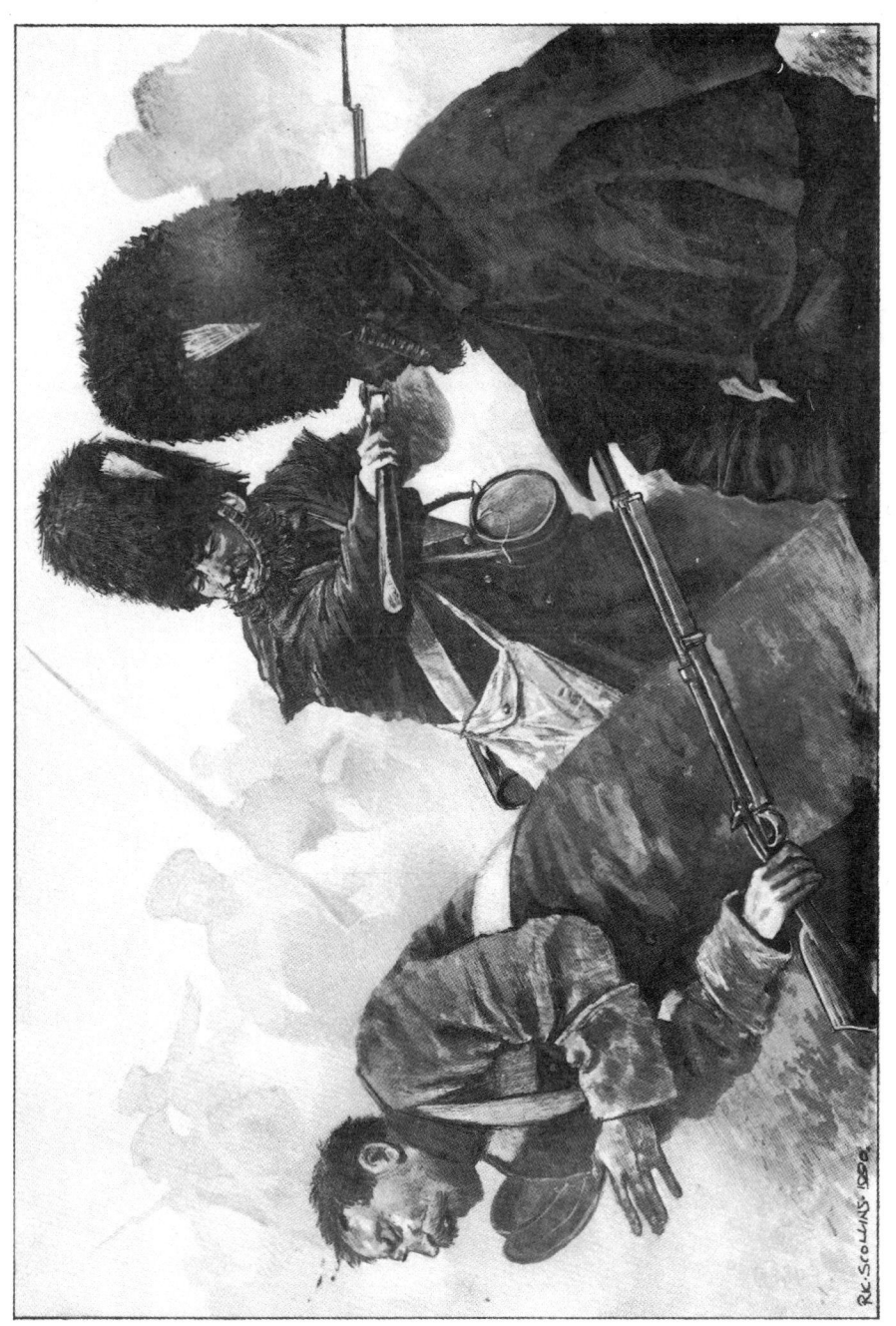

Storming the Great Redan, Sebastopol, 1855

The Relief of Delhi, 1857

Storming the Taku Forts, 1860

The Zulu War, 1879

The Broken Square at Abu Klea, 1884

The Battle of Omdurman, 1898

2 October Pontoko
  Ensign John T Down, 57th Regiment
  Drummer Dudley Stagpoole, 57th Regiment

20 November Rangiriri
  Assistant-Surgeon William Temple, Royal Artillery
  Lieutenant Arthur F Pickard, Royal Artillery

11 February 1864 Mangapiko River
  Major Charles Heaphy, Auckland Militia

30 March Te Awamutu
  Lieutenant-Colonel John C McNeill, 107th Regiment

29 April Gate Pah, Tauranga
  Captain of the Foretop Samuel Mitchell, Royal Navy
  Assistant-Surgeon William G N Manley, Royal Artillery

21 June Tauranga
  Captain Frederick A Smith, 43rd Regiment
  Sergeant John Murray, 43rd Regiment

24 January 1865 Nukumara
  Captain Hugh Shaw, 18th Regiment

JAPAN

6 September 1864 Straits of Simono Seki
  Midshipman Duncan G Boyes, Royal Navy
  Captain of the After Guard Thomas Pride, Royal Navy
  Seaman William H H Sealey, Royal Navy

INDIA

30 April 1865 Dewan Giri, Bhootan
  Major William S Trevor, Bengal Engineers
  Lieutenant James Dundas, Bengal Engineers

CANADA

9 June 1866 Danville Station, Quebec-Montreal Railway
  Private Timothy O'Hea, Rifle Brigade

GAMBIA

30 June 1866   Jubabecolong, Barra
Private Samuel Hodge, 4th West India Regiment

BAY OF BENGAL

7 May 1867   Little Andaman Island
Assistant-Surgeon Campbell M Douglas, 24th Regiment
Private David Bell, 24th Regiment
Private James Cooper, 24th Regiment
Private William Griffiths, 24th Regiment
Private Thomas Murphy, 24th Regiment

ABYSSINIA

13 April 1868   Magdala
Drummer Michael Magner, 33rd Regiment
Private James Bergin, 33rd Regiment

INDIA

4 January 1872   Lalgnoora, Looshai
Major Donald Macintyre, Bengal Staff Corps

ASHANTE

17 January 1874   Abagoo
Major Reginald W Sartorius, 6th Bengal Cavalry

31 January   Amoaful
Lance-Sergeant Samuel McGaw, 42nd Highlanders

4 February   Ordalsu
Lieutenant Mark S Bell, Royal Engineers

February   Becquah
Lieutenant, Lord Edric F F Gifford, 24th Regiment

PERAK

20 December 1875   Malacca
   Captain George N Channer, Bengal Staff Corps

INDIA

27 April 1877   Quetta, Beluchistan
   Captain Andrew Scott, Bengal Staff Corps

SOUTH AFRICA

29 December 1877   Draaibosch, near Komgha
   Major Hans G Moore, 88th Regiment

SOUTH AFRICA

22 January 1879   Isandlwana, Zululand
   Lieutenant & Adjutant Teignmouth Melvill, 24th Regiment
   Lieutenant Nevill J A Coghill, 24th Regiment
   Private Samuel Wassall, 80th Regiment

22/23 January   Rorke's Drift, Natal
   Lieutenant John R M Chard, Royal Engineers
   Lieutenant Gonville Bromhead, 24th Regiment
   Corporal William W Allen, 24th Regiment
   Private Frederick Hitch, 24th Regiment
   Private A Henry Hook, 24th Regiment
   Private Robert Jones, 24th Regiment
   Private William Jones, 24th Regiment
   Private John Williams, 24th Regiment
   Surgeon James H Reynolds, Army Medical Department
   Assistant-Commissary James L Dalton, Commissariat & Transport Corps
   Corporal Ferdnand C Schiess, Natal Native Contingent

12 March   Ntombe River, Zululand
   Sergeant Anthony C Booth, 80th Regiment

28 March   Hlobane Mountain, Zululand
   Lieutenant-Colonel Redvers H Buller, 60th Rifles
   Major William Knox-Leet, 13th Regiment
   Lieutenant Edward S Browne, 24th Regiment

Sub-Lieutenant Henry Lysons, 90th Regiment
Private Edmund J Fowler, 90th Regiment

3 July White Mfolozi River, near Ulundi, Zululand
Captain, The Hon. William L de La P Beresford, 9th Lancers
Captain H Cecil D D'Arcy, Frontier Light Horse
Sergeant Edmund O'Toole, Frontier Light Horse

SOUTH AFRICA

8 April 1879 Moirosi's Mountain
Sergeant Robert G Scott, Cape Mounted Rifles
Trooper Peter Brown, Cape Mounted Rifles

5 June Moirosi's Mountain
Surgeon-Major Edmund B Hartley, Cape Mounted Rifles

SOUTH AFRICA

28 November 1879 Sekhukhune's Town
Private Thomas Flawn, 94th Regiment
Private Francis Fitzpatrick, 94th Regiment

AFGHANISTAN

2 December 1878 Peiwar Kotal Pass
Captain John Cook, Bengal Staff Corps

31 January 1879 Peshawar
Lieutenant Reginald C Hart, Royal Engineers

17 March Maidanah
Captain Edward P Leach, Royal Engineers

2 April Futtehabad
Lieutenant Walter R P Hamilton, Bengal Staff Corps

21 April Kam Dakka
Captain O'Moore Creagh, Bombay Staff Corps

24 October Shahjui
Captain Euston H Sartorius, 59th Regiment

11 December   Killi Kazi
The Reverend James W Adams, Bengal Ecclesiastical Department

13 December   Sherpur Cantonment, Kabul
Lieutenant William H Dick-Cunningham, 92nd Highlanders

14 December   Koh Asmai Heights, Kabul
Lance-Corporal George Sellar, 72nd Highlanders
Captain Arthur G Hammond, Bengal Staff Corps
Captain William J Vousden, 5th Punjab Cavalry

27 July 1880   Maiwand
Sergeant Patrick Mullane, Royal Artillery

28 July   Maiwand Road
Gunner James Collis, Royal Artillery

16 August   Deh Khoja, Kandahar
Lieutenant William St L Chase, 28th Native Infantry
Private Thomas E Ashford, 7th Regiment

1 September   Kandahar
Major George S White, 92nd Highlanders
also 6 October 1879 – Charasiah

INDIA

22 November 1879   Konoma, Naga Hills
Captain Richard K Ridgeway, Bengal Staff Corps

SOUTH AFRICA

14 January 1881   Sepachele Village, Tweefontein
Surgeon John F McCrea, Cape Mounted Yeomanry

SOUTH AFRICA

16 January 1881   Elandsfontein, Transvaal
Lance-Corporal James Murray, 94th Regiment
Trooper John Danaher, Nourse's Transvaal Horse

28 January   Laing's Nek, Natal
Lieutenant Alan R Hill-Walker, 58th Regiment
Private John Doogan, 1st Dragoon Guards

22 February Wesselstroom, Transvaal
Private James Osborne, 58th Regiment

27 February Majuba Hill, Natal
Lance-Corporal Joseph J Farmer, Army Hospital Corps

EGYPT

11 July 1882 Alexandria
Gunner Israel Harding, Royal Navy

5 August Kafr Dowar
Private Frederick Corbett, King's Royal Rifle Corps

13 September Tel-el-Kebir
Lieutenant William H M Edwards, Highland Light Infantry

SUDAN

29 February 1884 El Teb
Captain Arthur K Wilson, Royal Navy
Quartermaster-Sergeant William Marshall, 19th Hussars

13 March Tamai
Lieutenant Percival S Marling, King's Royal Rifle Corps
Private Thomas Edwards, Black Watch

NILE EXPEDITION

17 January 1885 Abu Klea
Gunner Alfred Smith, Royal Artillery

UPPER BURMA

1 January 1889 Lwekow, East Karenni
Surgeon John Crimmin, Bombay Medical Service

4 May Tartan
Surgeon Ferdinand S Le Quesne, Army Medical Service

INDIA

27 March 1891   Manipur
   Lieutenant Charles J W Grant, Indian Staff Corps

INDIA

2 December 1891   Nilt Fort, Hunza-Nagar
   Captain Fenton J Aylmer, Royal Engineers
   Lieutenant Guy H Boisragon, Indian Staff Corps

20 December   Nilt Fort
   Lieutenant John M Smith, Indian Staff Corps

GAMBIA

17 March 1892   Toniataba
   Lance-Corporal William J Gordon, West India Regiment

BURMA

6 January 1893   Simla, Kachin
   Surgeon-Major Owen E P Lloyd, Army Medical Service

INDIA

3 March 1895   Chitral Fort
   Surgeon-Captain Harry F Whitchurch, Indian Medical Service

MATABELELAND

30 March 1896   Bulawayo
   Trooper Herbert S Henderson, Rhodesia Horse, Bulawayo Field Force

22 April   Bulawayo
   Trooper Frank W Baxter, Grey's Scouts, Bulawayo Field Force

MASHONALAND

19 June 1896   Mazoe Valley
  Captain Randolph C Nesbitt, Mashonaland Mountain Police

INDIA

26 July 1897   Malakand
  Lieutenant Edmond W Costello, Indian Staff Corps

INDIA

17 August 1897   Nawa Kili, Upper Swat
  Lieutenant, Viscount Alexander E M Fincastle, 16th Lancers
  Major Robert B Adams, Indian Staff Corps
  Lieutenant Hector L S McClean, Indian Staff Corps

INDIA

16 September 1897   Bilot, Mohmand Valley
  Lieutenant James M C Colvin, Royal Engineers
  Lieutenant Thomas C Watson, Royal Engineers
  Corporal James Smith, East Kent Regiment

INDIA

20 October 1897   Dargai Heights, Tirah
  Piper George Findlater, Gordon Highlanders
  Private Edward Lawson, Gordon Highlanders
  Lieutenant Henry S Pennel, Sherwood Foresters
* Private Samuel Vickery, Dorsetshire Regiment
  * also 16 November 1897 – Warah Valley, Tirah

SUDAN

2 September 1898   Omdurman
Captain Paul A Kenna, 21st Lancers
Lieutenant, The Hon. Raymond H L J de Montmorency, 21st Lancers
Private Thomas Byrne, 21st Lancers

2 September   Khartoum
Captain Neville M Smith, 2nd Dragoon Guards

22 September   Gedarif-Kassala
Captain, The Hon. Alexander G A Hore-Ruthven, Highland Light Infantry

CRETE

6 September 1898   Candia
Surgeon William J Maillard, Royal Navy

SOUTH AFRICA

14 & 27 October 1899   Mafeking
Captain Charles Fitzclarence, Royal Fusiliers
also 26 December 1899 – Mafeking

21 October   Elandslaagte
Captain Matthew F M Meiklejohn, Gordon Highlanders
Sergeant-Major William Robertson, Gordon Highlanders
Captain Charles H Mullins, Imperial Light Horse
Captain Robert Johnstone, Imperial Light Horse

30 October   Ladysmith
2nd Lieutenant John Norwood, 5th Dragoon Guards

11 December   Magersfontein
Corporal John D F Shaul, Highland Light Infantry
* Captain Ernest B Towse, Gordon Highlanders
Lieutenant Henry E M Douglas, Royal Army Medical Corps
* *also 30 April 1900 – Mount Thaba*

15 December   Colenso
Captain Hamilton L Reed, Royal Artillery
Captain Harry N Schofield, Royal Artillery
Corporal George E Nurse, Royal Artillery
Captain Walter N Congreve, Rifle Brigade

Lieutenant Frederick H S Roberts, King's Royal Rifle Corps
Private George Ravenhill, Royal Scots Fusiliers
Major William Babtie, Royal Army Medical Corps

26 December   Game Tree Hill, Mafeking
Sergeant Horace R Martineau, Protectorate Regiment
Trooper Horace E Ramsden, Protectorate Regiment

5 January 1900   Colesberg
Lieutenant, Sir John P Milbanke, 10th Royal Hussars

6 January   Wagon Hill, Ladysmith
Lieutenant James E I Masterson, Devonshire Regiment
Lieutenant Robert J T D Jones, Imperial Light Horse
Trooper Herman Albrecht, Imperial Light Horse

6 January   Caesar's Camp, Ladysmith
Private James Pitts, Manchester Regiment
Private Robert Scott, Manchester Regiment

18 February   Paardeberg
Sergeant Alfred Atkinson, Green Howards
Lieutenant Francis N Parsons, Essex Regiment

23 February   Hart's Hill
Private Albert E Curtis, East Surrey Regiment

24 February   Plowman's Farm, near Arundel
Sergeant James Firth, Duke of Wellington's Regiment
Lieutenant Edgar T Inkson, Royal Army Medical Corps

27 February   Pieter's Hill
Captain Conwyn Mansel-Jones, West Yorkshire Regiment

13 March   Koorn Spruit, Bloemfontein
Sergeant Henry W Engelheart, 10th Royal Hussars

31 March   Sannah's Post, Koorn Spruit, Bloemfontein
Major Edmund J Phipps-Hornby, Royal Artillery
Sergeant Charles E H Parker, Royal Artillery
Driver Horace H Glasock, Royal Artillery
Gunner Isaac Lodge, Royal Artillery
Lieutenant Francis A Maxwell, Indian Staff Corps

20 April   Wakkerstroom
Lieutenant William H S Nickerson, Royal Army Medical Corps

22 April   Wakkerstroom
Corporal Henry C Beet, Sherwood Foresters

20 May   Crow's Nest Hill, Doornkop, Johannesburg
Corporal John E McKay, Gordon Highlanders

2 June   Delagoa Bay Railway, near Pretoria
Corporal Frank H K Irby, Royal Engineers

26 June   Lindley
Private Charles Ward, King's Own Yorkshire Light Infantry

5 July   Wolve Spruit
Sergeant Arthur H L Richardson, Lord Strathcona's Corps

11 July   Lechochoek, near Krugersdorp
Captain William E Gordon, Gordon Highlanders
Captain David R Younger, Gordon Highlanders

24 July   Vredefort
Captain Neville R Howse, New South Wales Medical Staff Corps

2 August   Msilikatsi Nek
Private William House, Royal Berkshire Regiment

7 August   Essenbosch Farm
Sergeant Brian T Lawrence, 17th Lancers

21 August   Vanwyksvlei
Sergeant Henry Hampton, King's (Liverpool) Regiment
Corporal Henry J Knight, King's (Liverpool) Regiment

23 August   Geluk Farm, Leowkloof
Private William E Heaton, King's (Liverpool) Regiment

27 August   Bergendal
Private Edward Durrant, Rifle Brigade

1 September   Warmbaths
Lieutenant Guy G E Wylly, Tasmanian Imperial Bushmen
Private John H Bisdee, Tasmanian Imperial Bushmen

13 October   Geluk Farm, Leowkloof
Major Edward D Brown, 14th King's Hussars

20 October   Zeerust
Lieutenant Alexis C Doxat, Imperial Yeomanry

7 November   Komati River
Lieutenant Hampden Z C Cockburn, Royal Canadian Dragoons
Lieutenant Richard E W Turner, Royal Canadian Dragoons
Sergeant Edward J G Holland, Royal Candian Dragoons

22 November   Gibraltar Hill, Dewetsdorp
Private Charles T Kennedy, Highland Light Infantry

13 December   Nooitgedacht, near Pretoria
Sergeant Donald Farmer, Cameron Highlanders

7/8 January 1901   Monument Hill
Private John Barry, Royal Irish Regiment

28 January   Naauwpoort
Farrier-Major William J Hardman, 4th New Zealand Contingent

6 February   Bothwell Camp
Sergeant William B Traynor, West Yorkshire Regiment

24 February   Strijdenberg
Corporal John J Clements, Rimington's Guides

3 March   Derby
Lieutenant Frederick B Dugdale, 5th Royal Irish Lancers

16 May   Brakpan
Lieutenant Frederick W Bell, West Australian Mounted Infantry

18 May   Lambrechtfontein
Lieutenant & Adjutant Gustavus H B Coulson, King's Own Scottish Borderers

15 June   Thaba 'Nchu
Sergeant James Rogers, South African Constabulary

3 July   Vlakfontein
Lieutenant William J English, 2nd Scottish Horse (Dragoons)

4 July   Springbok Laagt, near Ermelo
Private Henry G Crandon, 18th Hussars

13 August   Ruiterskraal
Sergeant-Major Alexander Young, Cape Police

17 September   Blood River Poort
Lieutenant Llewellyn A E Price-Davies, King's Royal Rifle Corps

26 September   Itala
Driver Frederick H Bradley, Royal Artillery

30 September   Moedwil
Private William Bees, Sherwood Foresters

23 November   Geelhoutboom
Lieutenant Leslie C Maygar, Victorian Mounted Police

18 December   Tyglerskloof Spruit
Surgeon-Captain Thomas J Crean, Imperial Light Horse

20 December   Tafelkop
Shoeing-Smith Alfred E Ind, Royal Artillery

8 February 1902   Vlakfontein
Surgeon-Captain Arthur Martin-Leake, South African Constabulary

CHINA

24 June 1900 Peking
Captain Lewis S T Halliday, Royal Marine Light Infantry

13 July Tientsin
Midshipman Basil J D Guy, Royal Navy

ASHANTE

6 June 1900 Dompoassi
Sergeant John Mackenzie, Seaforth Highlanders

30 September Obassa
Captain Charles J Mellis, Indian Staff Corps

NIGERIA

24 March 1903
Lieutenant Wallace D Wright, Queen's Royal Regiment (West Surrey)

SOMALILAND

6 October 1902 Erego
Captain Alexander S Cobbe, King's African Rifles

22 April 1903 Daratoleh
Captain John E Gough, Rifle Brigade
Captain William G Walker, Bikanir Camel Corps
Captain George M Rolland, Berbera Bohottle Flying Column

19 December Jidballa
Lieutenant Herbert A Carter, Indian Mounted Infantry

10 January 1904 Jidballa
Lieutenant Clement L Smith, Duke of Cornwall's Light Infantry

TIBET

6 July 1904 Gyantse Jong
Lieutenant John D Grant, 8th Gurkha Rifles

An Analysis of Victorian VC Citations

I have carried out a comprehensive study of Victoria Cross citations published in the *London Gazette* from 24 February 1857 to 24 January 1905. I then compiled a list showing the total number of VCs awarded for each single action. This revealed the three superlatives to be:
20 VCs at the Great Redan, Sebastopol, Crimean War, 18 June 1855
17 VCs at the Sikandar Bagh, Lucknow, Indian Mutiny, 16 November 1857
12 VCs at the Great Redan, Sebastopol, Crimean War, 8 September 1855

The Great Redan, Sebastopol

During the Crimean War, Sebastopol was besieged by Allied forces for almost a year. It was heavily bombarded, and the Allies gradually worked their way towards it by constructing a series of trenches and tunnels. Two of the town's most powerful defences were a stone fortress called the Malakoff Tower, and the Great Redan, a structure of earthworks constructed as the Allies advanced. In an attempt to break the deadlock, British forces stormed the Redan early on the morning of 18 June 1855, as French troops simultaneously assaulted the Malakoff. The attacks failed with dreadful loss of life. On 8 September 1855 a new attack was launched. The Russians were forced to abandon the defences and the Allies entered Sebastopol.

The following are relevant sections from citations in the *London Gazette* which make reference to the recipient having taken part in the actions at the Great Redan on 18 June and 8 September 1855.

18 June

1. Captain William Peel, Naval Brigade
'...On 18 June 1855, for volunteering to lead the ladder party at the assault on the Redan, and carrying the first ladder until wounded.'
(London Gazette: 24 February 1857)

2. Midshipman Edward St J Daniel, Naval Brigade
'For devotion to his leader, Captain Peel, on 18 June 1855, in tying a torniquet on his arm on the Glacis of the Redan...' *(LG: 24 February 1857)*

3. Commander Henry J Raby, Naval Brigade

4. Captain of the Forecastle John Taylor, Naval Brigade

5. Botswain's Mate Henry Curtis, Naval Brigade
'On 18 June 1855, immediately after the assault on Sebastopol, a soldier of the 57th Regiment, who had been shot through both legs, was observed sitting up and calling for assistance. Climbing over the breastwork of the advanced sap, Commander Raby and the two seamen proceeded upwards of seventy yards across the open space towards the salient angle of the Redan, and... succeeded in carrying the wounded soldier to a place of safety...' *(LG: 24 February 1857)*

6. Gunner & Driver Thomas Arthur, Royal Artillery
'...Volunteered for, and formed one of, the spiking party of Artillery at the assault on the Redan, on 18 June 1855.' *(LG: 24 February 1857)*

7. Lieutenant Gerald Graham, Royal Engineers
'...Determined gallantry at the head of a ladder party at the assault on the Redan, on 18 June 1855...' *(LG: 24 February 1857)*

8. Captain Howard C Elphinstone, Royal Engineers
'For fearless conduct, in having, on the night after the successful attack on the Redan, 18 June 1855, volunteered to command a party of volunteers, who proceeded to search for and bring back the scaling ladders...' *(LG: 2 June 1858)*

9. Colour-Sergeant Peter Leitch, Royal Engineers
'For conspicuous gallantry in the assault on the Redan, 18 June 1855...'
(LG: 2 June 1858)

10. Sapper John Perie, Royal Engineers
'Conspicuous valour in leading the sailors with the ladders to the storming of the Redan, on 18 June 1855...' *(LG: 24 February 1857)*

11. Lieutenant William Hope, 7th Regiment
'After the troops had retreated on the morning of 18 June 1855, Lt W Hope, being informed...that Lt Hobson was lying outside the trenches badly wounded, went out to look for him...towards the left flank of the Redan...' *(LG: 5 May 1857)*

12. Private Matthew Hughes, 7th Regiment
'...On 18 June 1855, he volunteered to bring in Lt Hobson, who was lying severely wounded...' *(LG: 24 February 1857)*

13. Corporal Philip Smith, 17th Regiment
'For repeatedly going out in front of the advance trenches against the Great Redan, on 18 June 1855... and bringing in wounded comrades.'
(LG: 24 February 1857)

14. Captain Thomas Esmonde, 18th Regiment
'For having, after being engaged in the attack on the Redan, on 18 June 1855, repeatedly assisted...in rescuing wounded men from exposed situations.'
(LG: 25 September 1857)

15. Private John J Sims, 34th Regiment
'For having, on 18 June 1855, after the regiment had retired into the trenches from the assault on the Redan, gone out into the open ground...and brought in wounded soldiers...' *(LG: 24 February 1857)*

16. Sergeant William McWheeney, 44th Regiment
'...Volunteered for the advance guard...in the Cemetery, Redan, on 18 June 1855.'
(LG: 24 February 1857)

17. Colour-Sergeant George Gardiner, 57th Regiment
'...For unflinching and devoted courage in the attack on the Redan, 18 June 1855...'
(LG: 2 June 1858)

18. Sergeant John Park, 77th Regiment
   '...Remarked for determined resolution at both attacks on the Redan.'
   (LG: 24 February 1857)

19. Private John Alexander, 90th Regiment
   'After the attack on the Redan, on 18 June 1855, went out of the trenches under very heavy fire, and brought in several wounded men.'
   (LG: 24 February 1857)

20. Lieutenant John S Knox, Rifle Brigade
   '...Volunteered for the ladder party in the attack on the Redan, on 18 June 1855...'
   (LG: 24 February 1857)

8 September

1. Captain Gronow Davis, Royal Artillery
   'For great coolness and gallantry in the attack on the Redan, 8 September 1855...'
   (LG: 23 June 1857)

2. Sergeant Daniel Cambridge, Royal Artillery
   'For having volunteered for the spiking party at the assault on the Redan, 8 September 1855...'
   (LG: 23 June 1857)

3. Corporal John Ross, Royal Engineers
   'Intrepid and devoted conduct in creeping to the Redan, on the night of 8 September 1855, and reporting its evacuation...'
   (LG: 24 February 1857)

4. Lt-Colonel Francis F Maude, 3rd Regiment
   'For conspicuous and most devoted bravery on 8 September 1855, in the assault on the Redan...'
   (LG: 24 February 1857)

5. Private Joseph Connors, 3rd Regiment
   'Distinguished himself most conspicuously at the assault on the Redan, 8 September 1855...'
   (LG: 24 February 1855)

6. Assistant-Surgeon Thomas E Hale, 7th Regiment
   'For remaining with an officer who was dangerously wounded, in the fifth parallel, Redan, 8 September 1855, and for a second act of gallantry on 8 September 1855.'
   (LG: 5 May 1857)

7. Lieutenant Luke O'Connor, 23rd Regiment
   '...Behaved with great gallantry in the assault on the Redan, 8 September 1855...'
   (LG: 24 February 1857)

8. Assistant-Surgeon Henry T Sylvester, 23rd Regiment
   'For going out on 8 September 1855, in front of the fifth parallel right attack, to a spot near the Redan...'
   (LG: 20 November 1857)

9. Corporal Robert Shields, 23rd Regiment
   'For volunteering, on 8 September 1855, to go out to the front of the fifth parallel, after the attack on the Redan...'
   (LG: 24 February 1857)

10. Sergeant John Park, 77th Regiment
'...Remarked for determined resolution at both attacks on the Redan.'
(LG: 24 February 1857)

11. Ensign Andrew Moynihan, 90th Regiment
'At the assault on the Redan, 8 September 1855, he personally encountered and killed five Russians.' *(LG: 24 February 1857)*

12. Brevet-Major Charles H Lumley, 97th Regiment
'For having distinguished himself highly by his bravery at the assault on the Redan, 8 September 1855...' *(LG: 24 February 1857)*

Sikandar Bagh, Lucknow

Twenty-four Victoria Crosses were awarded for deeds at Lucknow, on 16-17 November 1857. The troops involved were the 4th Infantry Brigade, consisting of the 93rd Highlanders, 56th Light Infantry, 4th Punjab Rifles, and detachments of the 84th Regiment, 90th Light Infantry, the Madras Fusiliers and the Bengal Artillery.

As the British advanced they attacked a number of masonry fortresses, including a large stone compound called the Sikandar Bagh, which contained about 2000 rebels. The soldiers took part in more than one sectional assault, and therefore the VC citations have tended to generalise, announcing some of the awards as being for gallantry at 'Lucknow', with no reference to the individual actions. Only seven of the twenty-four VCs gained for the 2nd Relief of Lucknow were given for a specific action other than the storming of the Sikandar Bagh.

The following are relevant sections from citations in the *London Gazette* which make reference to the recipient having taken part in the action at the Sikandar Bagh (Secundra Bagh) or Lucknow, on 16 November 1857. I have provided explanatory notes where necessary.

1. Lieutenant Alfred K Ffrench, 53rd Regiment
'For conspicuous bravery on 16 November 1857, at the taking of the Secundra Bagh, Lucknow...' *(LG: 24 December 1858)*

2. Sergeant-Major Charles Pye, 53rd Regiment
'For steadiness and fearless conduct under fire at Lucknow... *and on every occasion when the Regiment has been engaged.' *(LG: 24 December 1858)*
*The 53rd Regiment took a major part in the Sikandar Bagh action.

3. Private James Kenny, 53rd Regiment
'For conspicuous bravery at the taking of the Secundra Bagh, Lucknow, on 16 November 1857...' *(LG: 24 December 1858)*

4. Private Charles Irwin, 53rd Regiment
'For conspicuous bravery at the assault on the Secundra Bagh, Lucknow, on 16 November 1857...' *(LG: 24 December 1858)*

5. Captain, The Hon. Augustus HA Anson, 84th Regiment
'...At Lucknow at the assault of the Secundra Bagh, on 16 November 1857...'
(LG: 14 December 1858)

6. Major John C Guise, 90th Regiment
'For conspicuous gallantry in action on 16 and 17 November 1857, at *Lucknow.'
(LG: 24 December 1858)
A footnote in the Regimental History (p 278) states that Major Guise was awarded the VC for gallantry 'at the attack on the Sikandar Bagh in November 1857.'

7. Sergeant Samuel Hill, 90th Regiment
'For gallant conduct on 16 November 1857, at the storming of the Secundra Bagh, Lucknow...' *(LG: 24 December 1858)*

8. Colour-Sergeant James Munro, 93rd Highlanders
'For devoted gallantry at Secundra Bagh, Lucknow, on 16 November 1857...'
(LG: 8 November 1860)

9. Lance-Corporal John Dunlay, 93rd Highlanders
'...On 16 November 1857, entered one of the breaches in the Secundra Bagh, Lucknow...' *(LG: 24 December 1858)*

10. Private Peter Grant, 93rd Highlanders
'For great personal gallantry on 16 November 1857, at the Secundra Bagh, Lucknow...' *(LG: 24 December 1858)*

11. Private David Mackay, 93rd Highlanders
'For great personal gallantry in capturing an enemy's colour... at the Secundra Bagh, Lucknow, on 16 November 1857.' *(LG: 24 December 1858)*

12. Private John Smith, Madras European Fusiliers
'For having been one of the first to try and enter the gateway on the north side of the Secundra Bagh, Lucknow, on 16 November 1857...' *(LG: 24 December 1858)*

13. Lieutenant Hastings E Harington, Bengal Artillery

14. Rough-Rider Edward Jennings, Bengal Artillery

15. Gunner Thomas Laughnan, Bengal Artillery

16. Gunner Hugh McInnes, Bengal Artillery

17. Gunner James Park, Bengal Artillery
'Elected for conspicuous gallantry at the *Relief of Lucknow, from 14 to 22 November 1857.' *(LG: 24 December 1858)*
The Bengal Artillery bombarded the Sikandar Bagh before the main assault began.

A RORKE'S DRIFT MAN

'Our last meal before the battle was eaten just as the swift darkness fell. I am sure that the spirits of not a few sank with the sun, because the solemn thought came that for some of us the sun had set for ever.'

Private Robert Tutt, RMLI, a veteran of the battle of Tel-el-Kebir, 1882

The Zulu nation had defied,
At Isandlwana a thousand soldiers died.
When the dreadful fight was done,
The raging Zulus hurried on.

As they advanced the soldiers stationed at Rorke's Drift,
Were building barricades so scanty and makeshift.
Four-thousand warriors came storming into view,
The Twenty-Fourth of Foot were ready, standing to!

They battled on throughout the night,
Staunch defenders had to stand and fight.
With bullet, bayonet, butt and hack,
They drove each fearful onslaught back.

The morning light revealed too many brave men dead,
Tired mortals bathed in blood the Zulu foe had shed.
Breech-loading rifles played their part with deadly verve,
True deeds of valour, and a steady British nerve.

As the nineteenth century moved into its fifth decade, Ireland was becoming dangerously overpopulated. There was little money, and poor people worked as labourers for landlords and tenant farmers, who provided them with a cabin in which to live, and a patch of land from which they scraped a bare subsistance. The potato was their only nutritious food, but in 1845 blight reduced the crop to a putrid slime. In the years that followed there were two partial and three complete failures of the potato crop. The result was the Great Famine, the worst natural disaster to hit the British Isles since the Black Death. There was 'total annihilation' from starvation and disease. Landlords found themselves near bankrupt because their destitute tenants could not produce their rent, and anxious to turn the land over to pasture they began a merciless campaign of eviction. To add to the terrible hardship there was political unrest as the Young Ireland movement were agitating for repeal of the Act of Union. Vast numbers of people were driven out of Ireland to North America to escape the misery of the 'doomed and starving island.'

It was into this turbulent environment that Henry Edward Gallagher was born, circa March 1855, of a poor Roman Catholic family, in the parish of Killenam, Thurles, County Tipperary. Thurles is a market town on the bank of the River Suir, near the Dublin to Cork road and rail route. St Patrick's Diocesan College was established there in 1837, and the Roman Catholic cathedral was completed on the site of an old Carmelite foundation in 1857. Henry's father was a farmer, but the lack of a nourishing diet brought scurvy, typhus and dysentery, and his parents were victims of disease. The Catholic church took over the farm and raised Henry as an orphan. He was taught to read and write, and when his working life began he gained employment as a clerk.

Another means of salvation for young Irish men was to travel to England to join the British Army. Even in those early days of the Victoria Cross, Thurles could boast a local hero. As a twenty-seven year old Assistant-Surgeon serving with the 90th Regiment, William Bradshaw had gained the VC for attending to wounded soldiers under fire, during the relief of Lucknow, Indian Mutiny, 26 September 1857. He returned to Thurles soon afterwards, where he died in 1861. He was buried in St Mary's churchyard, and a memorial dedicated to his name has been erected. Another memorial tablet in the same church is dedicated to Corporal John Cunningham, who was born in Hall Street, Thurles, in 1890. He gained the Victoria Cross while serving with the Prince of Wales's Leinster Regiment during the Great War in France in 1917. Sadly, he was killed in action four days after his deed.

At the age of nineteen, Henry Gallagher ran away and caught a ship bound for Liverpool. On 13 March 1874, he enlisted for the 25th Brigade of the British Army, and three days later he passed the medical. His enlistment papers state that he was 5 feet 6½ inches tall, with a chest measurement of 35 inches. He had amber eyes, dark-brown hair and a fresh complexion. General remarks refer to him as being 'exemplary, regular and temperate.' He was given the Regimental number 81, and he attested at the new depot in Brecon, South Wales, for twelve years service with the 24th (Warwickshire) Regiment of Foot. He was assigned to 'B' Company of the 2nd Battalion.

Army life was tough and disciplined, and young recruits had to mature into men very quickly. Henry took his turn on fatigues and guard duty, and there was drill and inspection on the parade ground. Each company lived, ate and slept in the same barrack room, which developed staunch loyalty to the unit. Wages were a shilling a day, with half deducted for extra rations and laundry. A soldier who served the Colours for twenty-one years was entitled to a pension. The Victorian army owed its existence to the Empire, which it policed and guarded at outposts in all parts of the globe.

Henry settled well into army routine and became a good soldier. He was made lance-corporal on 11 March 1875, and on 19 May 1875 the unit moved to Dover Citadel. On 14 December 1875, Henry gained a 2nd Class Certificate of Education. He was appointed corporal on 1 April 1876, and lance-sergeant on 17 January 1877. On 17 April 1877 he married Carolina Maria Stanley, who was aged seventeen. On 31 June 1877 the Battalion moved to Chatham, and on 9 October 1877 Henry was promoted to sergeant.

After four years of Home service the 2nd Battalion received orders to go to South Africa. On 1 February 1878 they embarked on the troopship *Himalaya* at Plymouth, to prepare for the wearisome month-long voyage, in cramped conditions. On arrival at the Cape their landing at East London on surf boats proved to be a dangerous operation, and by 14 March they had been ferried by train to King William's Town in the north-eastern Cape. The region was mountainous, and was intersected by deep ravines and rocky bush.

Sergeant Gallagher found South Africa to be a country as strife-torn as his own. The 1st Battalion, 24th Regiment, had been in South Africa since 1874, dealing with unrest among various native peoples, and the British had now become involved in a dispute between the Gaika and Gcaleka tribes, which was the ninth in a series of minor disturbances known as Cape Frontier Wars. The campaign followed the usual pattern of native warfare in the area. The rebels used the bushy terrain around the foot of Mount Kempt for refuge and extended lines of troops entered the scrub to flush them out. By June the Gaika and Gcaleka chiefs had been put out of action and the rebels lost heart. These sweeping skirmishes gave the 2nd Battalion their first experience of active service, and the Commander in Chief, Lord Chelmsford, complimented them on the 'admirable manner' in which they had performed their duties.

The 2nd Battalion arrived in Pietermaritzburg, Natal, on 6 August, and in December 1878 British forces began to make their way towards the border with Zululand, to prepare for a confrontation with the defiant Zulu king, Cetshwayo, and his army of highly disciplined and ruthless warriors. The plan of action was to invade Zululand in three main columns and make for the royal kraal at Ulundi. The 24th Regiment made up the bulk of the troops of the 3rd (Central) Column. On 9 January 1879, as they advanced towards the border, the long convoy of Regular infantry, colonial volunteers, and transport vehicles came over a hill, and two thatched buildings which made up the small mission station known as Rorke's Drift came into view. It was a place Henry Gallagher and his comrades would remember for the rest of their lives.

America beckons from across the sea as an Irish peasant and his starving family are hounded by creditors. At the time of Henry Gallagher's birth thousands had left their homeland, never to return.

Colour-Sergeant Henry Edward Gallagher – A Rorke's Drift Man. The photograph was taken in 1882, prior to his sailing to India.

Family tradition has it that Sergeant Gallagher was in charge of the defenders at the south barricade for the initial fighting at Rorke's Drift. He was later stationed in the mealie-bag redoubt.

Defending the hospital at Rorke's Drift.

A well-known photograph of the survivors of 'B' Company, believed to have been taken at Pinetown. Wounded soldiers such as Corporal Allen and Private Hitch are not present, but Sergeant Gallagher can be seen lying down on the front row, third from left.

Colour-Sergeant Gallagher's South Africa Medal (clasp: 1877-8-9) and Indian General Service Medal (clasp: Burma 1887-9). They had been the property of a private trust in Luxembourg when they came up for auction at the Westbury Hotel in south London, on 4 December 1991. They are now owned by a private collector in Manchester. Gallagher's Meritorious Service Medal, issued in 1911, is believed to be with a member of the family in New Zealand.

Caroline Lillian Gertrude Gallagher, the mother of Major Edward Lane, RE (retired), who is Henry Gallagher's oldest surviving grandchild. She was known as 'Lily' throughout her life, to distinguish her from her mother, who shared the same name.

Henry Edward Gallagher, junior, who became a Captain in the Royal Engineers. He is said to have been the mirror-image of his father.

The 24th Regiment Old Comrades at Aldershot on the 30th anniversary of Rorke's Drift, 1909. Henry Gallagher is on the third row from the front, sixth from right, and Fred Hitch VC, can be seen seated on the front row, fourth from left.

A close up of Henry Gallagher and Fred Hitch enhanced from the previous photograph. They are wearing caps.

A Gallagher family photograph taken on the occasion of the marriage of William Gallagher in 1911. Lily and her husband, Josiah Lane, are not present, but Henry's other children are:

Lawrence – back row, third from right; Henry – middle row, far right; William – the groom, centre of middle row; Daisy – middle row, second left; and Violet – front row, seated second left. Henry's sons became officers in the Royal Engineers, and his daughters married military men. Lawrence was the last surviving child when he died in 1985.

A close up of Henry and his wife enhanced from the previous photograph. Lily died in 1933 and is buried with her husband.

Wistaria
Augustine Road
Drayton Hants
30th March, 31

My dear Doll

Many thanks for your Box of old Ireland which we received on St Patrick's Day. Sure it was myself that felt a great man with it stuck in my hat when going up the hill wish that you had been with me and we should have taken all by storm, both Nana, Vi, & self, were pleased to hear from your chum that you were going on alright but sorry that your chum has had a shift, a well never mind keep it at present all at Drayton are quiet here but the weather is not to our liking very cold and wild, but I suppose that you get plenty of the same, we heard from Willie a short time ago he appears to be doing some sight seeing in Ind... we also heard from Stan about a fortnight ago he has been da

A letter written by Henry Gallagher on St Patrick's Day, 1931, a few months before his death. Henry and his grandson, Edward, who he knew as 'Doll' because of his appearance as a baby, had a good relationship and they wrote to each other regularly.

Henry Gallagher's grave after the funeral at Christ Church, Portsdown Hill, Cosham, in 1931. The floral tributes include wreaths from various ranks of the South Wales Borderers, and one from Charles Hitch.

The army had commandeered the buildings, turning one into a storehouse and the other into a field hospital. They set up camp between the storehouse and a large hill called the Oscarberg, which overlooked the garrison from the south. Beyond the mission station the ground sloped down to the Buffalo River, which formed the border between the province of Natal and the kingdom of the Zulus.

Cetshwayo had been issued with a harsh ultimatum. He did not respond in a satisfactory way, so hostilities began when British forces moved across the river into Zululand on the morning of 11 January 1879. The first skirmish with the enemy took place next day, and after being delayed for more than a week while tracks were constructed, a base camp was established on the foot of a strange flat-topped feature known as Isandlwana, thirteen kilometres from the border.

The men of 'B' company, under Lieutenant Gonville Bromhead, were disgruntled when they were told to remain behind to guard the outpost. However, more troops were moving up with the line of supply and they expected to rejoin the regiment soon.

As Sergeant Gallagher and his comrades looked out from their tents on the morning of Wednesday, 22 January 1879, it is unlikely they envisaged the momentous events that were to happen that day. Lieutenant John Chard of the Royal Engineers was in charge of a small party of maintenance men who were repairing one of the ponts at the river. He had been ordered to take his men forward to the base camp, and when he returned at lunch time he reported to Major Spalding, who was in charge of the sector, that Zulu forces had been seen in the area and action seemed imminent. As there was no immediate cause for alarm, the Major decided to go to Helpmekaar to hurry forward a unit of the 24th Regiment which was two days overdue. He departed at about 14-00 hours, leaving Lieutenant Chard in overall command at the post.

After lunch Sergeant Gallagher, in the company of Colour-Sergeant Frank Bourne, and three other NCOs of the 24th Regiment, went walking on the hills behind the post. They heard the pounding of artillery guns coming from the direction of Isandlwana, and as they looked across the hills towards the base camp they could see clouds of smoke. However, Isandlwana was eight kilometres distant, making it difficult to see clearly with the naked eye. They returned to the depot and reported what they had witnessed.

By this time the mid-afternoon sun was bearing down on them. Lieutenant Bromhead and some other officers had propped-up a sheet of tarpaulin as a form of heat shield, and they were relaxing under it. At about 15-00 hours a mounted infantryman came galloping into the post and immediately reported to the officers. His appearance and attitude prompted questioning looks from the men. The officers listened in disbelief as the panic-stricken trooper gasped out the news that the camp at Isandlwana had been taken by the Zulus and all the men left in it had been massacred. The dreadful report was confirmed by four colonial troopers who arrived with a note written by one of the few officers who had escaped from Isandlwana. Suddenly, a look of great urgency came onto Lieutenant Bromhead's face when he learned that, with British forces in disarray, a wing of the Zulu army was at that very moment on its way to attack Rorke's Drift – which they were to hold at all costs!

Bromhead at once sent a man down to the river to alert Chard. The officers were well aware of the precarious situation, but after a hurried consultation it was decided that they should stand and fight. There was a good supply of building material in the store from which to construct a barricade, such as grain-filled bags and wooden biscuit boxes.

As Sergeant Gallagher helped to move the bags and boxes one can only imagine how he must have felt. They had no idea of the strength of the force that was coming against them, or how soon they would be attacked. If they did not complete the perimeter before the Zulus arrived it would be impossible to keep them out. If it was possible at all! Armed with their short stabbing spears, Zulus were a ruthless foe, who gave no mercy and expected none for themselves. The young Irishman was placed in charge of the south wall, where two wagons had been included in the barricade, and several sharpshooters had been posted. A troop of mounted volunteers had made a welcome addition to the number of defenders, but at about 16-30 hours shots rang out from behind the Oscarberg which prompted a mass desertion of colonials. This left 139 men to defend the post, of whom nearly one in four had been hospital patients that morning.

Three days after the battle Lieutenant Chard wrote an official report which described the events that happened:

'I saw that our line of defence was too extended for the small number of men now left, and at once commenced an inner entrenchment of biscuit boxes, out of which we had soon completed a wall two boxes high, when, about 4.20 pm, five or six hundred of the enemy came in sight around the hill to the south. They advanced at a run against our south wall, but were met by a well-sustained fire; yet, notwithstanding heavy loss, they continued to advance 'till within fifty yards of the wall, when their leading men encountered such a hot fire from our front, with a cross one from the store, that they were checked. Taking advantage, however, of the cover afforded by the cook-house and ovens, they kept up thence heavy musketry volleys; the greater number, however, without stopping at all, moved on towards the left round our hospital, and thence made a rush upon our north-west wall and our breastwork of mealie-bags. After a short but desperate struggle those assailants were driven back with very heavy loss into the bush around our works. The main body of the enemy close behind had meantime lined the ledge of rocks and filled some caves overlooking us at a distance of 100 yards to the south, from whence they kept up a constant fire. Another body, advancing somewhat more to the left than those who first attacked us, occupied a garden in the hollow of the road and also the bush beyond it in great force, taking especial advantage of the bush, which we had not time to cut down. The enemy was thus able to advance close to our works, and in this part soon held one whole side of the wall, while we on the other kept back a series of desperate assaults which were made on a line extending from the hospital all along the wall as far as the bush. But each attack was most splendidly met and repulsed by our men with the bayonet. Corporal Schiess of the Natal

Native Contingent, greatly distinguished himself by conspicuous gallantry. The fire from the rock behind our post, though badly directed, took us completely in reverse, and was so heavy that we suffered very severely, and at six pm were finally forced to retire behind the entrenchment of biscuit boxes.

All this time the enemy had been attempting to force the hospital, and shortly afterwards did set fire to the roof. The garrison of the hospital defended the place room by room, our men bringing out the sick who could be moved before they retired. Privates Williams, Hook, R Jones, and W Jones, 24th Regiment, were the last four men to leave, holding the doorway against the Zulus with bayonets, their ammunition being quite expended. From want of interior communication and the smoke of the burning house, it was found impossible to carry off all the sick, and, with most heartfelt sorrow and regret, we could not save a few poor fellows from a terrible fate.

Seeing the hospital burning, and desperate attempts being made by the enemy to fire the roof of our stores, we now converted two mealie-bag heaps into a sort of redoubt, which gave a second line of fire all along, Assistant Commissary Dunne working hard at this, though much exposed; thus rendering most valuable assistance.

Darkness then came on. We were completely surrounded, and after several furious attempts had been gallantly repulsed, we were eventually forced to retire to the middle and then to the inner wall of our kraal on the east of the position we first had. We were sustaining throughout this a desultory fire kept up all night, and several assaults were attempted, but always repulsed with vigour, the attacks continuing until after midnight, our men firing with the greatest coolness, not wasting a single shot. The light afforded by the burning hospital proved a great advantage. At four am, on 23 January firing ceased; and at daybreak the enemy were passing out of sight over the hill to the south-west. About eight am, however, the British Third Column appeared, and at sight of this the enemy, who had been gradually advancing towards us, commenced falling back as our troops approached.'

In his official report Chard estimated that about three thousand Zulus had attacked, of whom three hundred and fifty were killed. The battle left fifteen defenders dead, two dying, and ten wounded. Chard remarked: 'Of the steadiness and gallant behaviour of my whole garrison I cannot speak too highly.' Lieutenants Chard and Bromhead were awarded the Victoria Cross, as were Corporal Allen, and Privates Fred Hitch, Henry Hook, John Williams, Robert Jones and William Jones, all of the 24th Regiment. This remains the most VCs gained by one regiment for a single action in British military history. VCs were also awarded to Surgeon James Reynolds, Commissary James Dalton and Corporal Schiess. Major Edward Lane, RE (retired), Gallagher's grandchild, states:

'HE Gallagher, my grandfather, gave graphic pictures of the defence of Rorke's Drift and the way in which 'B' Company withstood the attacks so fearlessly. He remembered the initial horror felt at the sight of the first wave of the attack as so many Zulus in battle array came down on them. But as the fighting progressed all fear left him because he was so busy shooting. He was in charge of the south wall of bags and wagons, and was later stationed in the mealie-bag redoubt. All the defenders were in a state of collapse when the fighting was done. He carried the scars of the defence with a permanent blue mark on the right side of his nose, which was a powder burn caused by the backflash each time he fired his rifle.'

The trauma of battle suffered by the defenders had a deep affect on them and many soldiers discharged from army service soon after the war. Henry Gallagher chose to remain with the Colours, as one of the veterans who came to be easily recognised by admiring comrades as 'A Rorke's Drift Man.'

The invasion had suffered a serious reverse. But the British simply licked their wounds, requested reinforcements, and prepared to take their revenge. The fit men of 'B' Company remained at Rorke's Drift until mid-April, suffering harsh conditions. They had to sleep out in cold and sometimes wet weather, with no change of clothing or comforts of any kind. Many men were victims of disease, and at one time Lieutenant Chard was close to death. The 24th Regiment were deeply disappointed not to have taken part in the battle of Ulundi on 4 July 1879, when the Zulus were finally defeated. In August they moved to Utrecht in the Transvaal, where Major Bromhead and Private Robert Jones received their Victoria Crosses. Having received orders to go to Gilbraltar, the unit arrived in Durban to prepare for embarkation. Each Rorke's Drift defender was presented with a scroll of honour and a commemorative bible, in recognition of their 'heroic defence of Natal.' On 13 January 1880 they set sail for the Mediterranean aboard the troopship *Orantes*.

The 2nd Battalion, 24th Regiment, arrived in Gibraltar, where the most active events seem to have been the occasion when the 2nd Battalion received new colours, and Private John Williams was presented with the Victoria Cross. They arrived back in Brecon on 3 December 1880, and on 26 January 1881, Henry Gallagher was promoted colour-sergeant. In July that year the regiment was renamed the South Wales Borderers, and Colour-Sergeant Gallagher was given the regimental number 1590.

Home service brought a happy occasion for Henry and Caroline Gallagher, when their first child, Caroline Lillian Gertrude, was born on 17 August 1881. Colour-Sergeant Gallagher remained at Brecon when the 2nd Battalion left for Bombay in August 1882, but he joined his unit on 3 January 1883, with his wife and daughter. They did not set foot in Britain again for ten years. Four more children were born while the family were abroad. They were Henry Edward – born at Secunderabad on 17 June 1883; William Alfred – born at Madras on 13 October 1885; Violet Elizabeth – born at Toungoo, Burma, on 29 August 1888; and Daisy Dorothea – born at Ramkhet on 10 February 1890.

The Battalion had been stationed at Poona, Secunderabad and Madras, when they received orders to go to Burma, on 8 May 1886. Thibaw, the king of Burma, had been showing much anti-British feeling for many years. In 1885 a British force advanced up the Irrawaddy River and occupied Mandalay in a swift, almost bloodless campaign, which became known as the 3rd Burmese War. Upper Burma was annexed to the British Crown, to be administered as a province of India. However, the Burmese army refused to surrender, and took refuge in the vast jungle, from where they launched a campaign of guerilla warfare. Dacoit bands set out to disrupt the everyday life of the occupying British. In 1886 they twice set fire to Mandalay, and British troops were faced with the massive task of pacification, while protecting British interests. The following is an extract from a first-hand account by Colour-Sergeant Edward J Owen, Hampshire Regiment, who served in Burma at the same time as Colour-Sergeant Gallagher:

> 'We had conquered Mandalay and taken it, but we had not quelled the Burmese, who set to work to worry us, and succeeded amazingly well.
>
> Gangs of Decoits broke into the city, in spite of all our precautions, and killed people, and set fire to places, and scurried off before even their presence was known. The buildings were mostly made of wood and bamboo, and burnt fiercely when they were once alight, especially as there were practically no fire appliances. Sometimes several acres were destroyed before the flames were conquered.
>
> The Decoits used to slip in and out at night, seldom trying their luck in the daytime, for they had a holy dread of British rifles. They were positively merciless, and for some time after the occupation of the city it was unsafe to move about singly. No men were allowed to go outside the walls unless properly armed, and in parties of at least three.
>
> Mandalay was very unhealthy, and I was glad when I was ordered away to chase Decoits, though I should have thought better of it if I had known what the work really meant. For eighteen months I was away from civilisation, marching through a country where no proper roads existed, and thinking that I had done well if an average of ten miles a day had been covered.
>
> Decoit hunting in a hot, dangerous climate was hard work, with very little glory in it. We seldom got the enemy to close quarters, as he was so nimble, and the country so jungly. The robber-murderers had runs like rabbits, and it was almost impossible to follow them. It was woe indeed for the soldier who fell into their clutches.'

The tour of duty in Burma cost the South Wales Borderers more casualties from disease and sickness than from the enemy, and they were glad to get back to India. They served at the Bareilly and Ramkhet stations from 10 November 1888 to 19 October 1892, when Colour-Sergeant Gallagher embarked on the *Serapis* and set sail for a one year tour of Aden. They arrived six days later, and the soldiers immediately realised it was another unpleasant place. Henry spent forty-eight days in hospital from 2 July to 18 August 1893, having treatment for 'severe wear of the foot', before at last returning to India.

The Battalion arrived back in England on 18 November 1893, being stationed at Hilsea, and Gosport, Hampshire. On 28 February 1895, Colour-Sergeant Gallagher was permitted to continue his service beyond twenty-one years, and on 10 August

1895 he was appointed to the Army Staff as Garrison Sergeant-Major. The sixth and last child was born to the Gallaghers in Portsmouth, on 9 June 1895, and was named Lawrence Stanley. Henry's last tour of duty took him to Egypt from 28 September 1895 to 30 March 1897. Major Lane states:

> 'My mother, his oldest offspring, told me that when they were stationed in Egypt and he was Garrison Sergeant-Major, how particular he was in his 'turn out'. She was responsible that no blemish was visible on his red tunic, blue trousers, belt, and highly-polished boots, before he left their quarters for his daily duties throughout the garrison. I am sure he was the terror of any soldier who appeared to be idle or slovenly – in spite of his short stature.'

GSM Gallagher was discharged from the army at Gosport on 10 May 1897, after serving the Colours for 23 years – 56 days. He was awarded a pension of forty-one pence a day for life, although this changed several times during his retirement and he was receiving £102-15s-0d a year at the time of his death. He became Barrack Warden at Portsmouth, and made his home at a house called 'Wistaria' in Augustine Road, Drayton, Hampshire. Sadly, the house no longer exists.

Army Orders for January 1911 announced that Henry Gallagher had been awarded the Meritorious Service Medal. This medal was instituted by a Royal Warrant dated from 1845, and was created to be awarded to selected Warrant Officers or Sergeants who rendered distinguished or meritorious service. It is a silver disc bearing the effigy of the monarch on the obverse, and the inscription 'For Meritorious Service' on the reverse. The ribbon is crimson with white edges and centre. It carries a grant not exceeding twenty-pounds. Henry was awarded an annuity of ten pounds. Major Lane states:

> 'He retired from the army in 1897. I remember him from about 1919/20 until his death. During that period I regularly spent two or three weeks annually at his home in Augustine Road. He was very fond of his grandchildren, and we loved him. He had a great sense of humour and a real Irish sense of fun. When I first got to know him he would tell me stories of his soldiering, especially South Africa and Rorke's Drift in particular. He was proud of his Regiment, the Twenty-Fourth, and maintained his soldierly smartness and appearance all his life. He was a great story-teller on any subject true or fictitious. He was very fond of walking, especially on the Portsdown Hill. We would walk many miles on what he called 'campaigning', me asking questions, and he giving the answers – which I fully believed. But sometimes his deliberate exaggerations gave the clue that it was all his 'Irish blarney' coming out.
>
> He loved his small garden, where he grew most of his vegetables and kept chickens. He died very suddenly in 1931, when strangely, I was stationed with the Royal Engineers in Ireland, quite close to Thurles, and from where I kept up a corresondence with him.'

Henry Edward Gallagher died at his home on 17 December 1931, aged seventy-five. The cause of death was recorded as 'Cardiac Syncope' and 'Chronic Myocarditis'. He was buried with military honours in the cemetery at Christ Church, Portsdown Hill, Cosham, Hampshire.

There is no doubt that Henry Gallagher was a Rorke's Drift man. However, nothing much seems to have been recorded about his part in the defence, and he is rarely mentioned in the general literature on the subject. It has been written in one book about the battle that Major Lane has stated how he remembered Frederick Hitch VC visiting his grandfather. But Hitch died in 1913 so this is not possible. Nevertheless, Henry Gallagher and Fred Hitch were both members of the Old Comrades Club and would almost certainly have been friends. Therefore, the visitor Major Lane saw at Augustine Road may have been Hitch's son, Charles, who served with the South Wales Borderers, often sending floral tributes to the funerals of Rorke's Drift veterans. Major Lane states:

'On the anniversary of the defence of Rorke's Drift each year my grandfather requested to be left alone with his memories.'

VICTORIAN NAVAL BATTLES AND DISASTERS

'Why conceal the horrors of war? The more they are revealed the sooner will men sicken and say that war shall be no more.'

Private John Clarke, 59th Regiment, a veteran of the China Wars, 1856/60.

THE BOMBARDMENT OF ACRE, 1840

Seaman Francis Trevas, RN. *HMS Revenge*

The ancient fortress of St. Jean d'Acre, on the coast of Israel, is famous in history as the scene of many sanguinary conflicts. Richard the Lion-Heart and the Crusaders besieged it, with a loss that has been put as high as 300,000. A century later the Saracens retook the fortress, and 60,000 Christians perished. Napoleon repeatedly failed to capture it in 1799, and retreated. In 1840 the stronghold was occupied by the Egyptians under the rebel Viceroy, Mehemet Ali. He had overrun Syria, and the allied Powers of Europe intervened, headed by Great Britain. After a fierce bombardment the fortress surrendered and the Viceroy was defeated. The narrator of this story of one of the last great fights in which the old sailing ships of the British Navy took part is in his ninety-second year. He possesses a vivid recollection of the incidents of this memorable battle.

I can take you back a long way in history – not as far as Nelson, but to a battle in which one of the *Victory's* guns was fired time after time, in just the same way as it had thundered in Trafalgar Bay. That gun was on board the *Bellerophon* at the bombardment of Acre, and you may see it now at Greenwich Hospital.

Acre, too, was famous for being the first naval engagement in which steamers were used; but there was too much prejudice against them to give the craft a chance of showing what they could really do in battle.

I was one of the old school of seamen, and had no fancy for the queer, quaint paddle steamers, as they then were, which had been in the "Navy Lists" for ten years or so. The first was called the *Lightning*; but her speed would make a present-day seaman laugh. There were lots of the old ships of the line and frigates which could have run away from her in a good breeze.

The Forties were ticklish times in the Near East. The Pacha of Egypt, Mehemet Ali, had bottled up the Turkish Fleet at Alexandria, and he was defying the allied powers of England, Russia, Austria, and Prussia. He had France at the back of him, and it was known that if the allies were beaten France would fall on them instantly. That would have been a serious thing; because the French in the Mediterranean were in first-rate battle trim, while we were on the peace establishment. Those were the days when England and France didn't love one another. The British Commander-in-Chief in the Mediterranean, Admiral Sir Robert Stopford, and his commodore, Charles Napier, were officers of the days of Rodney, Howe, and Nelson, and the Navy, as I knew it, had not changed very much since the time of those great admirals.

One of the most wonderful of the old sea dogs was Napier, who was known in the Near East as the Great Commodore. He won the most marvellous victories on the Syrian Coast, so many that at last only the fortress of Acre remained to be dealt with.

The commodore was an artful customer – one of the real old school of fighting sailors. He was born, you know, in 1786, and was serving in the Navy as a first-class volunteer when Nelson was chasing the French and Spaniards over various parts of the globe. He dressed pretty much as Nelson was dressed at Trafalgar, and there was but little difference between our own ship and the *Victory*. Both were sailing vessels, and we fought at Acre just as they fought at Trafaglar, having nothing but the wind and our sails to depend on.

Napier was known all through the Navy as a brave and wonderfully eccentric officer. I used to see him with his cocked hat half turned round on his head and taking snuff in vast quantities. Most men, even in those snuff-taking days, were content to help themselves from an ordinary box; but the commodore wasn't an ordinary man, so he had a little pocket made on the outside of the breast of his coat, and he used to dig his thumb and fingers in and sniff up the stuff with a terrible relish. The blue of the cloth was turned quite brown with the snuff, and sometimes there wasn't much difference between the colour of the uniform and that of the commodore's features.

He was a fine, dashing tar, and we would follow him anyway, and do anything for him. There was no taking liberties. He laid down the law, and however little we liked it, we had to obey. They say that after he left the Navy he dressed in a more amazing fashion than ever, and that he wore shirt-collars with ballet-girls printed on them. Well, I never saw that, but, from what I did see of his dress, I can quite believe the story.

The ships were pretty much like the officers – links with the old fighting Navy which, since Navarino in 1827, had had a longer spell of peace than anybody cared for, because it was so bad for promotion and glory. The squadron that was sent under Napier against Acre consisted of the *Princess Charlotte*, the *Powerful*, the *Bellerophon*, the *Revenge* (which was my own ship), the *Thunderer*, the *Edinburgh*, and the *Benbow*, all ships of the line, with two frigates and four steamships. There were two Austrian frigates, an Arabian corvette, and a Turkish ship with a name that meant "the days of yore." Her captain was a British naval officer who had been lent to the Turkish Government to command their fleet.

It was on the afternoon of November 2nd that we anchored off the fortress of Acre, towards Mount Carmel. You see, we were in a region that we had all heard about in the days when we read the Bible. I had plenty to do with scriptural places during that commission of the *Revenge*, but I was very glad to see the last of them when the war was over.

Steamers were something of freaks in those days, and when it was proposed that they should tow the ships of the line in, the commodore objected, and showed that the big, bulking hulls would be exposed to the fire of the batteries, one by one, before they could reply with the full force of their own broadsides. Like the old sailor he was, he preferred the wind to steam, and eventually the squadron was anchored in two divisions, in about six fathoms of water.

The drums had beaten to quarters, and the battleships, frigates, and steamers were ready to bombard the fortress, which was supposed to be impregnable and unconquerable. Acre was in reality a terrifying place. It bristled with cannon; there were 147 in the sea batteries alone, to say nothing of the mortars; and the place had ammunition, stores, and provisions enough to last for a siege of ten years. There were about 4500 men in the garrison, and nearly 1000 cavalry were posted outside the city.

Wasn't it Wellington who said, after Waterloo, that every man who wore a uniform wasn't necessarily a hero? Well, the same remark applied to sailors in my own day, just as it always has applied and will, as long as men go to war. There were lots of officers and men who would rather have been tucked up snugly in bed ashore or tackling a gale of wind, than sailing up to the bombardment of Acre. Why, the very name of the stronghold stood for impregnability and bloodshed, and there were a good many in the fleet who thought it was certain death to engage the batteries.

Our own captain, a salt who had been in many battles and had lost an eye in one, was so badly upset that he could scarcely read the Articles of War to us; but the worst case I knew of was that of one of the gunners.

He got into such a mortal funk, owing to his belief that the ships could be blown out of the water, that he laid a train of gun-powder to the magazine, and it was only by luck that a marine, who was on sentry, saw the fuse in time, and it was put out.

When the gunner was found, he was dead, for he had cut his throat. He might just as well have waited for the enemy to finish him off; but the odd and humorous thing about it was that there was no fear of the Egyptians causing mischief to his ship, because by that time we had beaten them. The gunner's ship and another were sailing up to take part in the battle; but they were too late. That shows you what fear will do if you give way to it.

But all fear vanished as soon as the fight began, for then it was crash against crash, battleships against batteries.

One awful thing happened, which seemed to end the fight like magic – and well it might.

In the citadel there was an immense powder magazine, and this blew up with a noise louder than any thunder or bombardment I ever heard, and with a glare that was almost like all the lightning in the heavens flashing at once. The very earth shook, and in the ships we felt a concussion like a collision or striking a rock. Many of the seamen were hurled to the deck by the shock. The explosion was followed by a dreadful shower of ruins and rubbish and, worse still, shattered human beings. An entire battalion of Egyptians perished, and it was calculated that 2000 lives were lost as a result of the blowing up of the magazine. The fire of the ships accounted for a thousand more.

The noise was terrific, and the smoke became so dense that it was scarcely possible to see either man or ship or shore. In the low 'tween decks of the ships the gunners, nearly naked, fought just as they had fought not many years before at Trafalgar. Our shot and shell told heavily on the batteries, while we were so placed that the Egyptians could not hull or really damage us.

Most of their shots went high, and did mischief to our spars and rigging. The ships of the line and the frigates boomed away with their old muzzle-loaders, while the steamers sent shells screaming into Acre; and every shell caused ten times more havoc than the old-fashioned round shot.

In the citadel there was an immense powder magazine, and this blew up.

I do not think that in any case the bombardment would have lasted very long, because it was so tremendous, and the fortress was getting so badly damaged and the Egyptians so severely punished.

Can you wonder that after such a holocaust the Egyptians lost heart and surrendered? I was able to see them, when the battle-smoke had cleared off, running away like frightened women – they were dressed almost like women – and trying to seek shelter in the mountains. But most of them preferred to be prisoners in British hands rather than risk falling into the power of their cruel and tyrannic leaders.

I daresay you have often heard of men in battle being killed by the wind of a shot – the concussion and compression of the air as a shot or shell screams by. Some people say that such a thing cannot happen, but I know better, for I saw a case in the *Revenge*.

A little drummer was standing by the mainmast with his drum in front of him. A shot came from one of the batteries, crashed through the bulwarks of the ship, and smashed a piece out of one of the starboard guns before it went and buried itself in the sea. The shot rushed past the drummer, just grazing his breast, but not touching him. There he stood, drum in front of him, looking just as if he were waiting for the order to beat to quarters; yet he was dead, killed instantly by the wind of the shot that had not even scratched his skin. I saw him then, and I have so often seen him since in imagination. I call him back to mind now, here in sunny Dorsetshire, seventy years after I was fighting in the *Revenge* off the coast of Syria.

I saw some cruel and pitiful sights when I went ashore after the battle, the worst of all being the spectacle of whose who still lived after the magazine had exploded. The shock had been dreaful and the mischief terrible. The enemy had fled, leaving their dead and wounded. It would have been merciful if some of the injured had been killed outright, because their sufferings were unspeakable. Nothing I saw was more moving than the spectacle of a poor fellow whose face – the lower half – had been partly shot away, and who, in spite of his wounds, looked as if he were trying to speak, for the upper features were moving convulsively. He may have been asking for water, or he may have been praying to us to end his torture. We did what we could and passed on. Then came the time when we had to bury the dead. We dug a trench about two miles long, and in it we placed the men who had perished, putting them in rows of three, heel to heel.

Those were days of torture and suffering to thousands of poor Egyptians, who were forced to fight, whether they liked the game of war or not – and most of them had no relish for it. The Viceroy was a remorseless tyrant, and crafty, too, so that there was little chance of anybody getting the better of him. Egyptian mothers are like mothers all the world over – they would rather keep their sons at home than let them go away, especially to fight their country's battles. Mehemet wanted soldiers, and he forced all young men who were physically fit to serve in his army.

There was no escape from this service except by adopting measures from which all Christian mothers would shrink; but they were prepared to go to any length to get exemption, and many of them destroyed the sight of one eye in their children, so that they should not be able to use firearms. But the Viceroy was too artful to be

There he stood, drum in front of him, looking just as if he were waiting for the order to beat to quarters; yet he was dead.

checkmated like that, and he made the poor, mutilted children, when they were old enough, go into the army and learn to shoot with the eye that was left.

I saw great numbers of these one-eyed Egyptians both ashore, when we landed at Acre, and on board ship, when we were crowded with prisoners. It was a very pitiful spectacle; but I am sure the Egpytians were a great deal happier as captives under the British flag than they had been under their own banner. We had to knock about at sea with them on board till the weather got fine enough to allow us to land them – and when that happened, I don't know which side felt happier, the seamen or the prisoners. We were so densely packed on board that we could scarely move or breathe.

Many of us thought that when we got ashore at Acre we should have plenty of loot; but one of the first things we were ordered to do was to keep our hands off the Egpytians' things. We all obeyed, having no choice in the matter, and the only thing belonging to other people that we seized was shot.

Those were frugal times, and shot and shell were not turned out as they're made nowadays. It took a long time to fill up our magazines when once they'd been emptied – and we had pretty well cleared them out during the bombardment. When we got ashore, parties were told off to gauge and collect the shot we had fired from the ships.

I was the armourer's mate of the *Revenge,* and had a gauge with me – a primitive sort of ring on a stick. I put the gauge over any shot I came across, and if the ring fitted the shot it was ours, and was taken to the boats and sent to the ship.

Oh yes – other ships' shot fitted my gauge all right; but as I have told you, that was the only sort of loot we got at Acre. Besides, I daresay other crews stole our shot, so it worked out fairly enough, taking it all round. We put the shot back into the magazine, and there it was ready to be fired again.

I wonder what the sailors of to-day would say if they had to go after their own shot and pick it up and bring it back? But they'd have to go a wonderful long way for some of it, judging by what I hear of the immense distances that the big guns will carry. Why, any little modern fighting ship would have smashed us all off the water without getting so much as a scratch over the business.

France has been threatening and blustering, and one result of our victory was that there was no danger of war with her, as there would have been if we had been vanquished at Acre. A French ship was in harbour, and we went up and saluted her. By way of answer she saluted us – with the Union Jack turned upside down! That might easily have ended in bloodshed with a hot-tempered admiral like ours; but the French were kept bottled up till there had been time to send a steamer off to get an explanation, and for her to come back with apologies, and say that it was all a mistake and meant nothing. We had to wait a long time before we learnt this, for those were slow-moving days, when people did things more leisurely than they do now.

If that fight took place to-day you would know all about what happened – and a good deal more – in a few hours; but newspapers were very scarce in the Forties, and the first news my parents got of the battle was many weeks afterwards, when I landed back in England. Until I told them about it they did not know that there had been any such thing as the bombardment of Acre.

There cannot be more than one or two English survivors of that famous fight at Acre; not more than one or two who wear the riband for it. I should have had my medal – I was so proud of it, just as I am of this broad bit of silk – but, long years ago, I lent it to my daughter to play with, and she fastened it round the cat's neck. The cat ran out of the house, and from that day to this I have never seen the medal.

I wonder if it will ever come back to me?

RANGOON:
STORMING THE GOLDEN PAGODA, 1852

Seaman George Goddard, RN. *HMS Rattler*

A petty dispute led to the second Burmese War of 1852, a conflict which included the storming and capture of the famous Golden Pagoda at Rangoon. The war lasted two years, and ended in the addition of Pegu to our Indian Empire. Two British merchant captains had been fined by a Burmese court. They complained to the British authorities, and claimed compensation. The demand was refused, and a British expedition was sent to Rangoon in November, 1851, to enforce it. Rangoon, the maritime capital of the Burmese Empire, was taken by storm on April 14th, 1852, and in the following December was added to the British Empire. One of the very few survivors of the war is Mr. George Goddard, who was at that time an ordinary seaman, serving in H.M.S. "Rattler."

To talk about line of battle ships, powder-monkeys, screw-corvettes, and bow-chasers is to carry you back to the navy of more than fifty years ago. I am going to do that, because it is the only British Navy that I remember. As a boy I went into the *Prince Regent*, a sailing ship of the line; and afterwards I joined the *Rattler*, a screw-corvette of eleven guns, which was ordered out to the East, where they say the temple bells are ringing, and calling you back.

Well, I saw a good many temples, and they made a ringing noise, but not with bells particularly. They were guns in my time, and they flung their murderous chain-shot over the swampy rice-fields and the muddy Irrawaddy, and did their level best to smash the expedition that was sent to punish the Burmese. And the temple that made the biggest noise was the Golden Pagoda, a splendid gilded building which glowed in the terrific heat of the pitiless Indian sun.

The *Rattler* left Woolwich for Portsmouth at the end of 1851, but did not reach Rangoon until April 1852. The marvel is that she ever got to the East at all, for we ran into the worst gale I have ever known in English waters. We were three days getting from Woolwich to Portsmouth, and it was thought that we had foundered. Boats were smashed and spars carried away; but when we had refitted we were off again, to make Rangoon by way of Madeira, Sierra Leone, Ascension Island, St. Helena, the Cape, Singapore, and Moulmein.

The night before we reached Sierra Leone we were caught in a very heavy tornado, and many of our spars and sails were torn away. The thunder roared incessantly, and the vividness of the lightning was appalling. We put the helm up and put the ship before the wind, and on she went, dragging a mass of wreckage after her. I remember so well struggling up to the mainyard and trying to stow the canvas, which was ballooning out to such an extent that it seemed impossible to get at it. I really thought that not even the war to which we were going could be worse than this. Afterwards I should have been glad to exchange Rangoon for the tornado. We are never satisfied in this world.

At Moulmein there was an English garrison, and we took on board some troops. Lord Wolseley was in the war – the first of his many campaigns; and, for anything I know to the contrary, he may have embarked with us to go to Rangoon. But I do not remember. You see, in those days he would be an ensign, and naturally you don't expect an ordinary ensign to become Commander-in-Chief of the British Army. There are so many ensigns, and only one commander-in-chief.

We entered the Irrawaddy, and ascended the river till we got within sight of Rangoon. Then we anchored, and found ourselves in a river about as wide as the Thames at London Bridge. On each side of us were swampy rice-fields, with insignificant buildings shooting up from the low grounds.

Most noticeable of all the structures was the Golden Pagoda, which reminded me of nothing so much as St. Paul's at home, rising from a cluster of mean structures, and very near the river, too.

Rangoon was really a city of pagodas, terraced and fortified. Just as in London, from a high building, you can look round on almost numberless churches, with St. Paul's rising in splendid dignity above and dwarfing them, so, it seemed to me, you could look upon Rangoon, with its little temples and the biggest and most magnificent of them all, the Golden Pagoda.

It seems a hard thing to set yourselves deliberately to pound a temple with your guns, but that is what we had to do in the muddy Irrawaddy; and we had to do it because the Golden Pagoda was the most strongly fortified of all the places we had to deal with, and because the gunners who defended it set steadily to work to blow the *Rattler* out of the water. We offered a fine target; so did the Golden Pagoda. But we soon discovered that the structure was beyond the range of our guns. That was lucky for the Golden Pagoda, which in these days would be pounded to pieces in a few minutes.

The *Rattler* was light of draught, and so we had been able to steam up and take our place for the bombardment. In those days steamers were primitive concerns. I have seen engines positively lift themselves out of their beds at every revolution of the crank – and it took them all their time to look after themselves. But the sailing ships were worse; they were absolutely helpless, and so it happened that we had to take the frigate *Fox* in tow. We had to leave her, however, because her draught was too deep for the Irrawaddy. The *Fox* was a forty-four gun frigate, and flew the broad pennant of Commodore Lambert, who commanded the river expedition. I believe we cast the frigate off before we began the bombardment of the stockades which had been made to defend Rangoon – stockades of mud and cane and stone – a sort of strong fence to keep an enemy at bay. The stockades were loopholed, and from the embrasures peeped the muzzles of guns and muskets. I do not think that any gun they had was bigger than a 12-pounder, and those were the days, remember, of muzzle-loaders.

It was Easter Sunday, just before noon, when the Burmese opened fire upon us from their stockades. Then the fight began which meant an incessant pounding until sunset.

It was a steady, simple sort of battle; gun against gun; steam-corvette against joss-house.

Marvellous indeed is the change that has taken place in war. Nowadays you shut yourself up in walls of steel and pound away with weapons that are terrible to look upon and think about. When a ship goes into action not a living soul is seen; but guns, officers, and crew were just as visible on board the *Rattler* as a motor-'bus is in the Strand.

The captain and the first lieutenant were on the bridge; other officers, such as mates and midshipmen, were on deck; and the crew were on deck, too, for the most part, because the guns were on the upper, or spar deck, and the heaviest of them all was the 68-pounder in the bow – a pivot gun. We had five broadside guns and the pivot gun, in all eleven. The broadside guns, which were 32-pounders, were exactly the same sort of weapon as was used at Trafalgar.

We might, indeed, have been Nelson's sailors come to life again - many of them were still alive – for we had our powder-monkeys in the *Rattler*, just as the *Victory* had. These little fellows ran between the guns and the magazine hatchway and brought the powder in their cartridge-boxes. They looked on the business as a glorious game, and revelled in the fighting. I sometimes think that the youngsters of to-day are not made of the same stern, dare-devil stuff as the lads who were helping to pound the joss-houses. There are no powder-monkeys nowadays; hydraulic lifts and electric devices do their work. I should be utterly lost on board one of our modern battleships.

I was the assistant loader of one of the broadside guns and wore what we call a jumper – that is, a sort of white jacket, with white trousers and a white hat. It was the lightest clothing you could have, even for the tropics; yet it was too much, and many a man stripped to the waist long before the bombardment ended.

It was unsufferably hot, but we pounded away, fascinated by the sight of the mischief that we did. Our weapons were not formidable, but they were heavy compared with the Burmese guns, and we saw stockade after stockade destroyed, and exploded powder magazine after powder magazine.

On the bridge the captain watched Rangoon and the havoc of our shots. He gave his orders by word of mouth to the first lieutenant, who shouted them to the junior officers on deck, and they in turn controlled the captains of the guns. All was absolutely fair and above board; now, in our warships, the captain gets into the conning-tower, and with the help of his tubes and electric wires directs his ship just as the brain guides the human body.

One by one we shattered the stockades. Sometimes our broadsides blazed; then there was the deeper boom of the pivot gun and the roaring of the shot across the swampy rice-fields, mostly towards the Golden Pagoda. That was the chief target, because it was from the Golden Pagoda that the biggest shots came towards us. It was there that the Burmese had their heaviest guns, although those weapons, as I have pointed out, were not nearly so effective as our own.

Our shots went home with pitiless precision, but the Burmese cannonade was harmless. We had no casualties from the guns themselves – those came later, in the storming – but we suffered from the terrible sun. We had no small-arm fire, but our muskets, loaded, were ready for instant use, and we had our cutlasses buckled on, in the good old Trafalgar fashion, as we served the guns. We got very thirsty, of course, and helped ourselves to drinks from buckets of water which were placed about the deck.

The bombardment went on until nearly sunset; then Rangoon seemed to be burning, and it looked as if the Burmese had had enough of the *Rattler*. The bugle sounded the cease fire, and boats were manned and armed, and I went away in one of the cutters to disperse some of the enemy who had gathered on the bank of the river, rather too near to be agreeable. They had had enough of us, however, and bolted into the jungle; and I at any rate, had had enough of them for the time being, and was glad to see them go.

Next day two of the East India ships came up, the *Fermosa* and the *Pluto*, with troops on board and guns and ammunition. The guns were landed on the Monday and Tuesday by the simple method of throwing them overboard onto the mud. We had to get them out and clean them, so as to be ready for the storming of the Golden Pagoda. There were no artillerymen; all that particular work was done by the sailors.

With the Royal and East India troops leading the way, and the detachment from the Navy bringing up the rear with the guns, drawn by bullocks, we began the storming. I fancied that, as we had escaped in the ship, we should be lucky enough on shore to get clear of the shot; but it was a very different business indeed this time.

On the Easter Sunday the Burmese had only a ship to go at, and not a very big one, with weak artillery; now they could fire point-blank at masses of marching men, with chain shot – that is, shot chained together, and canister and grape shot, which means that the guns were loaded with bullets and pieces of metal which, when fired, scattered and did terrible mischief.

The Golden Pagoda is very much like one of the pyramids, crowned by a structure which looks like an enormous lighthouse, a gilt spire which you can see from every part of the surrounding country. All round the pagoda are smaller shrines, or temples, and in the fifties the building was moated and defended by batteries.

Standing on a small hill, which is the only high ground in the district, the pagoda was an unpromising fort to attack; but the stormers marched across the exposed land, under a burning sun, towards the moat and the drawbridges.

We sailors had the work of seeing to the guns, and a tough job it proved to be, for when the chain shot and the rest of the scrap-iron began to fly amongst us and cut us up, some of the bullocks fell, badly mangled. The other bullocks, maddened by the smell of blood and the awful noise which the whizzing iron made, either tried to bolt or, which was just as bad, refused to budge.

There we were struck, open to the full fury of the fire from the pagoda, unable to get the guns nearer because of the stubborn animals. All the same, we served the guns and smashed away at the enormous golden building. It was needful to get nearer, and we beat and pulled and cajoled; but the bullocks would not move; then our commanding officer, the first lieutenant, shouted to us to clear the animals out and drag the guns ourselves; and with plenty of cheering we obeyed and took the ropes and hauled the guns to a more suitable place.

The lieutenant was a magnificent specimen of the old fighting naval officer, the man whose trade was battle, and who did not know the meaning of fear. He saw what

Boats were manned and armed, and I went away in one of the cutters.

was happening; he noticed that some of us – myself amongst them – were ducking and bobbing our heads rather faster, I think, than the flying shot. You couldn't help it; for when you heard that murderous whizz you ducked instinctively. Shame didn't count. The lieutenant was standing on a bit of rising ground, with the scrap-iron whistling and whizzing about him, with his sword drawn, and, believe me, never moving a muscle. He scorned to do it.

"It's no use bobbing and ducking," he shouted at last. "You aren't going to save your skins' that way. Hold up to it, men, and face it! And plug in with the guns as hard as you can. The faster you fire, the sooner you'll be through with it."

So we did as we were ordered to do, and having dragged the guns up we pounded away at the Golden Pagoda and, to do them justice, the Burmese blazed away at us.

Ambulances began to come down from the pagoda and past us; but the most singular thing about them was that they contained men who had not been wounded, but had been struck down remorselessly by the sun, the heat of which was perfectly dreadful. More men died of the heat and disease during the war than were accounted for by either gun or musket or robber.

Being in the rear of the stormers I did not quite see all that was passing in front, where the soldiers were, but I saw them going ahead, and I saw them rush the moat and the drawbridges, and I saw the Burmese bolting across the rice-fields and the cornfields, leaving their guns and their Golden Pagoda behind them, and thinking only of one thing, and that was the best way of saving their skins.

At last, I scarcely knew how, I found that I was on the steps of the famous temple, and I sank exhausted by the heat and the desperate fighting. The dead and dying Burmese, who were around on every hand, in the moat, and on the level ground, showed how fierce the combat had been, and the passing ambulances and the red-clothed figures on the earth told the sorry tale of British loss. Yet even then I could not help noticing the magnificence of the great place, which is said to be the most splendid of all the Burmese temples.

All sorts of dragons and weird idols were around me, and there was a horror hidden in every dark place about the uneven stairs. I believe that even in these days, when British tourists go in perfect safety to the temple which I helped to take, they are awed into silence when they begin to make their way up the dark, uncanny by-ways to the building to look at it, or, like the Burmese, clap a patch of gold leaf on to add to its splendour, and at the same time, I fancy, to rid them of some of their sins.

There had been a lot of talk of loot. Wonderful stories have been told of the riches of the Golden Pagoda, of jewels in abundance, and of precious metals, which were to be had for the picking up. I believe that a good deal of treasure fell to the lot of some of the stormers, but I myself did not come across it; I certainly did not get a share of the riches. They went mostly to the troops; the sailormen were out of it, because they were in the rear. Besides, they were not quite so well up to the game as the soldiers of those days. I am talking now of the times when the old East India Company was in existence, and when soldiers in the East could make fortunes out of loot, and ships' captains make fortunes, too, out of two or three voyages.

On that famous night I slept on the steps of the Golden Pagoda. The night before I had camped out under the stars. I was none the worse for the fight. A spent ball had struck me in the stomach, but had not done lasting mischief. The Burmese kept up a ragged firing as they retired, which they had done very willingly, because the temple was a very sacred place and treasure house, and they did not want it to get into the hands of infidels, as I suppose they called us.

When morning came I went back to the ship, without seeing the inside of the pagoda; but I was not sorry on that account, because the heat was insufferable, and the mosquitoes were worse than the heat. They literally swarmed. It was no use killing them, for millions rose up to take the place of the slain. On board ship it was impossible to sleep for them, and my legs were swollen with their bites, to say nothing of my hands and face. I remember going below and passing my hand along one of the beams. It was wet and warm with the blood from the mosquitoes, which, after their feast, had got as far as the beam. You could sweep thousands of them away in a second.

No, there was no East calling me, once I had got away from it, and I don't think poets would answer the call so readily or listen so much to the temple bells if they had had the experience of Rangoon that came my own way in the early fifties. I daresay things are better in these days; but I suppose that the Golden Pagoda rises up now, as it did then, from the melancholy rice-fields and the dismal mud banks of the river, with their untold millions of shrimps.

We buried our dead and left the fallen Burmese to be looked after by their own people. Then we had to set to work to clear the country of the Burmese who had taken to dacoiting or robbing; and hot work it was, too, especially as the dacoits loved nothing so much as fooling us and then escaping.

We would track them so closely that we fell upon their very living-places; but as for the Burmese themselves I seldom saw them. Once enough, however, I was in time, with my comrades, for the dinner that the dacoits had made ready for themselves. Great pans of rice would be seen on the fire cooking and the chickens would be plucked ready for roasting. We finished the cooking and the roasting, and after that, with very contented minds, finished the dinner, too. So you see, it wasn't all chasing in vain.

I was thankful enough to leave the land of swampy rice-fields and pagodas and blood-thirsty mosquitoes and go farther East, this time to the China Seas after pirates, who swarmed in their junks and lurchers, which were bigger and faster craft than junks.

The pirates were cruel and pitiless. When we caught them in the beginning we handed them over to the Chinese authorities, who put them to death without mercy. I used to see the poor wretches crucified against walls, or with their eyes gouged out or their limbs mutilated. The authorities were even more merciless than the freebooters.

At last we got orders that the pirates were to be destroyed without mercy, ships and all, and that they were not to be captured. There were two reasons for this – first and foremost, humanity, because it was too terrible to hand them over to their own judges;

The men ... fell to work with the steel and boarded their junk in the good old reckless fashion.

and, secondly, because they were a constant menace to the peace and safety of the China Seas.

One day a naval officer and his boat's crew had made a valiant attack on some pirates. The men only carried ten rounds of ammunition, and these were soon exhausted; then they fell to work with the steel and boarded their junk in the good old reckless fashion, slashing at and sweeping away the pirates with the cutlass.

Those of the Chinese who escaped from the boarders ran away, and the lieutenant and his men followed them.

Instantly another junk, whose sweeps were got out, rowed steadily down towards the captured vessel, and the pirates swarmed on board. Hearing the noise, the officer and his men hurried back to the deck.

They were met with overwhelming numbers and the lieutenant and three men were killed on the spot, cut to pieces with spears, while the rest were hacked and left for dead. Some villagers found the poor wounded fellows, and brought them and the news of the disaster to us.

Being a steamer, we were soon on the track of junks and lurchers, and, the guns having done their work, we got the boats out, and boarded what were left after the fire and shot had done their duty. One day I and a comrade, cutlass in hand, had rushed below, after accounting for all the pirates, so far as we knew.

We were prodding about, trying to turn hidden Chinamen out of dark holes and corners, when we both started and, perhaps, turned rather pale. I, at any rate, felt uneasy enough, for on the deck we heard a most terrible and uncanny noise.

"I thought they were all done for!" explained my comrade. "She only carried a dozen men, and I fancied we'd settled 'em."

"There's more on deck," I answered.

In a brace of shakes we had rushed on deck.

We saw no Chinamen, but there, just by us, was the most enormous chest I ever set eyes on – a huge box about three feet deep, the same width, and something like ten feet long.

Chinamen are the most cunning creatures on two legs, and instantly I thought that we had a box full of the yellow devils, waiting for a chance to spring out at us.

For one awful moment we stared at the thing; then I whispered:

"Have you your musket ready?"

"Yes," he answered, and there was dew on his forehead which was not caused by the eastern sun.

"Then," I said, "I'll lift the lid up swiftly, and as soon as I do it shoot the first yellow man that jumps out. Then we'll slash in with the cutlass."

He presented his musket, and I jerked the lid up.

I fell back, and the lid fell back too, for the most affrighting yells and squeals greeted our ears.

The chest was full, not of Chinamen, but of pigs.

We carried out our orders, to fire and sink the lurcher, and I fear that a lot of fine roasted pork was wasted, because we had no time to shoot the tenants of the chest.

THE WRECK OF THE TROOPSHIP *BIRKENHEAD*, 1852

Corporal William Smith, 12th Foot

The *Birkenhead*, an iron paddle steamer of about 2000 tons, and 564 horse-power, sailed on January 7th, 1852, from Queenstown to the Cape, with drafts for various regiments – the 12th Lancers, and 6th, 12th, 43rd, 45th, 73rd, 74th, and 91st, and the 60th Rifles. She struck on a hidden pinnacle of rock called Danger Point, off Simon's Bay, South Africa. The rock ripped her hull, and in twenty minutes she broke in two and sank. Of 638 persons on board, mostly soldiers and sailors, 454 perished, only 184 being saved by the boats, a friendly schooner, and by rafts and bits of wreckage. The *Birkenhead* discipline is unforgetable, if only because of it every women and child was saved.

Corporal W. Smith, the fine old veteran on whose narrative this story of the *Birkenhead* is based, lives in a little village ninety miles from London. As a private in the 12th Foot, now the Suffolk Regiment, he embarked in the *Birkenhead* for active service in South Africa, and is one of the few survivors of this disaster. Corporal Smith served for eight years in the 12th, and fourteen years in the Cape Mounted Rifles. He was discharged in 1870 as a full corporal, with four good conduct badges. He served in no fewer than four campaigns in South Africa, including the Zulu War of 1879, and possesses three medals. He has a very small pension, but is not forgotten by the officers of his regiment, who are naturally very proud of him.

I am an old man – old in body, if you like, but young in memory and spirit, and I can still march with some of the best of them, in spite of my seventy-five years. I can recall many things that I did in my long years of soldiering on home and foreign service, and can picture many scenes that my eyes have witnessed.

But one event stands out with awful clearness, one memory will linger when all other impressions vanish, and I parade for the last muster – and that is, the picture of the sinking of the *Birkenhead*. From time to time the papers tell us that the only survivor of the troopship has died – that neither man or woman nor child who was in her when she struck on Danger Point, and broke her back and sank, is left; but some of us die hard, and there is still a handful of officers and men who were hurled into a shark-infested sea in the darkness of an early morning, and heard the last hopeless cries of soldiers as the steamer disappeared. Aye, and worse than that – the wails and screams of heartborken wives who had been torn from husband's arms, and the piteous cries of little children who were forced into the boats and rowed away, leaving to a sure and awful death those who were sacrificed that they might live.

The old King of Prussia commanded that the story of the *Birkenhead* drill and fortitude should be read to every regiment in his army; artists have painted pictures of the troops drawn up in steady ranks on deck, and poets have sung of the way the bugles rang and the drums beat; but there was no sound of bugle and no roll of drum; there was none of the stiffness of parade which pictures show – and yet there was a falling-in, a last muster, a standing shoulder to shoulder as the end came, and many a handshake and many a sobbed farewell. And how, at such a time, can even the bravest do otherwise, swept as they were swept, from perfect peace and comfort to an unexpected doom?

Sometimes, aye, often, I wake suddenly from sleep, or start up as I smoke in my little cottage in the quiet country, and wonder whether the vision that has come again is only dreaming or reality; and I have to take my papers out and cast my mind back over the half century before I am satisfied that I have not imagined it. The whole terrible catastrophe returns as fresh and vivid now as it was then – for such a thing as that makes the same scar in your memory as an ugly wound will leave upon your body – and I know what both are.

I am in the old regiment again, the 12th Foot, which became the Suffolk when it lost its number, and I am back in the early fifties, when the British soldier's duty was to obey every order, without wondering, as they do nowadays, why it was given and whether it was right. They were the days of iron discipline and not overmuch consideration for the private soldier, who was still only a machine for fighting purposes.

There is a strong draft of us of the 12th for the Cape, where we are going out to fight the Kaffirs, and there are drafts for other regiments – Lancers, Highlanders, and Rifles amongst them.

On January 7th, 1852, we embark in the *Birkenhead* and sail for the Cape. We are in a famous ship, for the *Birkenhead* is of big size for her day, and has already made the run to the Cape in forty-five days, while other vessels in the Navy have been as long as sixty-five. Think of that, you soldiers of to-day, who grumble because your steamer takes a month – but very rarely – to do the same distance.

But, after all, we are cooped up in a ship that is no bigger than many a fine ocean-going tug nowadays. She is not much more than two hundred feet long, but broad of beam and of nearly fifteen hundred tons. She has engines of 564 horse-power, and is of course driven by paddles. She has been made from a frigate into a steamer, and a heavy poop and forecastle have been added to her to increase her accommodation as a troopship. Even then we are packed like sardines in a box, and have to eat and sleep and get through the time as best we can, and trouble nothing about the many little comforts that we enjoy ashore.

We start at a bad time of the year, and after leaving Cork run into a lot of heavy weather which puts the crowning touch to our miseries afloat. Life and death are busy with us at sea, just as they ashore. The weary days go past, and the only thing that marks one from its fellows is a birth or death. One woman dies of consumption, and our spirits are depressed by the awful solemnity of her burial at sea. Three children are born – but at what a cost! Each mother dies – and what more striking evidence can you have of what it meant for women to sail in troopships fifty years ago?

The days pass slowly, and the *Birkenhead* steams steadily towards the south. Week follows week, and we have entered our seventh at sea when we are gladdened by the sight of Simon's Town. We reach it on February 23rd, after a voyage of forty-seven days. Now the weariness of the sea is forgotten and we are all alive with eagerness to reach the very end. Some, more lucky than the rest – how lucky they are so soon to learn – are landed, amongst them the handful of sick and more than half of the women and children. We learn definitely what we are to do, and find that the *Birkenhead* is to go at once to Port Elizabeth and East London, and that the drafts will join the forces of the Commander-in-Chief in South Africa, Sir Harry Smith, for service on the frontier of Cape Colony.

Who need describe the joyful expectation of those who fill the troopship? Not a man is there who does not burn to get ashore and march to the front, and there is not a soul who is not glad to think that there is only a pleasant little run along the coast before our long voyage is ended altogether. We are in perfect spirits as we steam out of Simon's Town at about five o'clock in the afternoon of February 25th.

How vividly that final run comes back again over the half century that has passed! The sea is calm and the night is clear, the daylight quickly fades and gives place to a glorious darkness. The lights are twinkling ashore, a grateful sight to us who have been so long surrounded by the tumbling seas. The stars, too, are shining brightly.

All is well.

From time to time as we thud bravely on from the Atlantic to the Indian Ocean we hear the sullen murmur of the surf which breaks ashore about two miles away, rising above the ever-present roar of the machinery which we no longer notice. A good lookout is kept, the leadsman is in the chains, and the watch on deck have little else to do but watch the lights glide past as the *Birkenhead* makes nearly ten miles an hour. The captain of the ship, Captain Salmond, has gone below, so has the commander, and the *Birkenhead* is in charge of Mr. Davies, second master.

I go below at last and turn in, never so much as thinking of danger. I discuss the latest news with my comrades. The gossip is that Captain Salmond is pressing the ship hard, for two reasons, one of which is that he wants to get ahead of the steamer *Styx*, which is carrying stores of war, and the other that he wishes to make a quick passage so that he can land the Commander-in-Chief, who is concentrating his forces for a grand attack upon the natives. And so that he may make his run as short as possible, Captain Salmond is keeping very near the coast.

We have gone to sleep on the crowded lower deck. Midnight has passed, one o'clock comes and goes, and the ship's bell strikes again. But I do not hear the strokes of the melancholy voice which rises in the night and proclaims that all is well. I am falling asleep and unconscious.

What is that? Why this appalling shock? Why these terrible cries, this sudden panic, this staggering confusion? Why are men crowding and struggling and all making, as if by instinct, for the campanion-ladder, to swarm on deck?

Why ask the question, for we know, even we who are landsmen, that the *Birkenhead* has struck; we know that even now some of her people are dead, drowned in their hammocks by the rush of the sea upon them.

I do what my fellow soldiers do, what nearly every soul on board does – struggle to the upper deck and clamour to know the worst. There are others like me, rushing up and crowding the deck - small space indeed for so many human beings. And it is dark, too.

On deck they are throwing the horses overboard.

What need to ask the question which the simplest soul on board can answer? The ship has struck on a sunken rock, and not even her water-tight compartments, of which she has no fewer than a dozen, can save her. The *Birkenhead,* with her resistless weight, driving hard, has been impaled upon a cruel, submerged fang, and she is ripped just as you might rip a drum of paper with your finger.

Panic, you ask? Confusion? Yes – both. And how can it be otherwise when, like a flash, sentence of death has been passed upon the *Birkenhead,* and in the twinkling of an eye serenity and safety have given place to overwhelming peril?

There are times when even the bravest of the brave succumb to their emotions. Was not the Iron Duke himself overcome with grief at the loss of so many of his troops at Waterloo? No wonder, then, that the men of the *Birkenhead* are in want of steadying when the first shock of the disaster falls upon them. Remember that most of them are very young – and then there are the men whose wives and children are on board. Put yourself in their places, then you will understand.

Even now, with the ship abruptly stopped, with the awful sound of rendering asunder in our ears, it seems impossible to believe that she is doomed. How can she be, the stout vessel that has borne us so far through such troubled waters without disaster of any sort? And so near the shore, too?

I know that even now, so far as I am personally concerned, there is no suspicion that the end will be what it proves to be. I see that things are bad; I am aware that already many lives are lost; but there are the boats, the coast is very close to us, and, above all things, there is the discipline – that spirit of all obedience which proves stronger than the love of life itself.

I have spoken of the panic, the confusion. They have been born suddenly, but their death is just as swift. Now come the exited voices of the officers – the men who are heard in the darkness, but are not seen.

It is "Steady, lads, steady!" and if there is a tremor in the tones – what of it? If at first, before the drafts have found themselves, there is something of a rush for the boats, what of that, either? Does not the panic die away at the word of command? Is not the rush stopped at the very onset? Do not the men make some pitiful attempt to fall in on that sloping deck, which is already breaking under their very feet?

And why? Because there are women and children on board, and the women and children are to be saved, whatever happens to the rest.

I seem to tell the story slowly; but however fast I spoke I could not do more than talk haltingly of a thing that happened with such fatal swiftness.

Lieutenant-Colonel Seton, of the 74th Highlanders, commanding the troops on board, gathers all the officers about him, and tells them at any cost order and discipline must be maintained. He specially charges Captain Wright of the 91st to see that Captain Salmond's instructions are obeyed, because on him alone, as a soldier, we can depend on safety.

Instantly sixty men are told off to work the chain-pumps on the lower deck, and I am one of the sixty. I go below again, and the stoutest heart might shrink from such a task. It is like descending into a dark well, for the water is already flooding the deck. But we strike out for the pumps, and in reliefs we man them and work with frantic energy. We might as well spare all our strength, because we do not make the least impression on the flood. How can we, with such a yawn in the troopship's side? She has been caught on the port side, between the foremast and the paddle-box, and the waves sweep in just like a heavy running stream.

We are up to our waists in water; but we work away at the pumps, cheering each other, saying that we shall soom be out of it and landed. But within touch of us are men drowned in their hammocks.

Officers are everywhere, steadying, encouraging, and directing. The rest of the troops are on the poop, and the women and children are there, too, drawn up in readiness to be put into one of the boats, the cutter.

Blue lights are burning, making a ghastly illumination in the darkness, and rockets crash on the stillness of the night. But no answer comes to our signals of distress. The lights are not seen, and the sound of rockets does not carry far.

What of the guns? you ask. Aye, guns would have boomed deeper, and could have been heard ashore; but we cannot fire them, because the ammunition is in the magazine, and the magazine is under water now, so that it is impossible to reach it.

Captain Salmond, like the brave commander he is, tries to repair his terrible mistake of hugging the coast too closely; and he forgets himself entirely in his wish to save his people – always the women and children first, remember. We hear his voice as he issues orders – orders – he swings a lantern in his hand – and we know that the engines, which are still workable, have been turned astern.

Fatal error again! and this time final. There is more hideous grinding, and tearing, and the rent in the hull is made bigger as the *Birkenhead* is backed. There is a mightier inrush of the sea, and a furious hissing as the boiler fires are drowned. But for the present we have no orders to leave our places, and we work unflaggingly at the useless pumps.

On deck they are throwing the horses overboard – the few officers' charges which the troopship carries; and the women and children are being driven and helped into the cutter. Can you understand what it means – that tearing away of wives and children from husbands and fathers – unhappy creatures who beg that they may die with their own loved ones rather than be saved without them?

Sixty men are at the chain-pumps, sixty more are struggling to lower the paddle-box boats. The other boats, too, are being handled.

What happens? The tackle is rotten, the boats themselves are ill-found and in bad condition, so that the very means by which alone we can hope for safety are not to be relied upon in our desperate extremity. In this furious effort to get the boats away, Mr. Brodie, the master, and a number of men are lost.

There is a long swell running towards the shore, and the *Birkenhead* is rolling heavily. Her foremast is tottering, her funnel is threatening to collapse. It leans dangerously over towards the starboard side, and as the fight with the boats goes on the smoke-stack thunders down and crushes a little host of human beings on the paddle-box.

Everything now happens with paralysing swiftness. The funnel has fallen – a great,

There is a piercing cry and a tingeing red of the sea—and the number of survivors is lessened.

high mass of metal; the foremast has come down, and the *Birkenhead* herself has snapped in two, her fore part dropping down into deep water and her stern tilting high in the air.

Half a hundred men perish instantly at the chain-pumps, and those who do not die rush up to the deck to hear the order given that all who can swim must jump overboard and make for the boats, which have got clear and are waiting at a safe distance so that they shall not be drawn into the water.

The order is given by Captain Salmond, but other voices are heard immediately – Captain Wright's and Captain Giradot's – begging that the men will stand fast, as the boats are full already with the women and children, and will be swamped if the soldiers make for them.

Discipline again! And always the women and children! The men stand fast, in the very grip of certain death, and not more than two or three jump overboard and try to reach the boat, which safely gets away.

During the whole of this time, the agonies of which no man can describe, Cornet Bond, of the 12th Lancers and Ensign Lucas, of the 73rd, have been superintending the removal of the women and children to the boat, and handing some of them to the gangway with a politeness and attention which is so wonderful that, sore as my own strait is, I cannot help smiling.

Cornet Bond, you say, is still alive – now Captain R.M. Bond Shelton – and you have met and talked with him? Then he has an old *Birkenhead* soldier's best wishes for continued life as a gallant officer and gentleman! Of Ensign Lucas I can speak myself, because I lived to serve under him. Here is a letter from him, sent to me only the other month, and a box of cigars, "for all old soldiers' smoke," he says.

Not twenty minutes have passed since we were sleeping peacefully and safely; now, with terrible noises, the troopship disappears, settling on the rock which has destroyed her, and with only her mainmast rising above the water.

For some minutes there is a scene which I cannot picture, there are sounds that I dare not recall; then there is something of quietness because the sea has claimed most of these desperate bidders for existence.

Where am I now? What new terror has been added to this great tragedy of a sailor's mistake?

I am overboard and in the water, clinging to a spar, a bit of wreckage which I have reached, I know not how. I have rushed on deck in my shirt and greatcoat, just as I have been roused from sleep, and in this clothing I am adrift in the Indian Ocean, a non-swimmer, and doomed to an eighteen hours' struggle in the sea to keep myself alive. I do not know that my fight will be for so long or so terrible, or I could never see it through; but I still have faith in my salvation, and grip my spar and look about for help.

And what do I see – what do I hear?

All around me are men who have been hurled to a pitiless death, some struggling fiercely, some clinging to any floating object from the wreck. There are awful sounds which I come to know well as the last groans or screams of men who sink to rise no more – and still more terrifying outbreaks which I do not for the moment understand, but the cause of which I quickly learn. They are the hopeless cries of victims who are seized and killed by sharks. Remember, we are in southern waters, in the southern summer, and the Indian Ocean thereabouts is swarming with these cruel monsters.

And yet, in all that time of suffering and terror, I am strangely undisturbed in mind. I cannot swim, but I have my spar to keep me up, and the knowledge that I am so near the land is wonderfully comforting and helpful. I have a feeling, too, that, having escaped so far, when so many have been swept to death, I shall be saved at last – and this conviction grows upon me even as the number of my comrades lessens.

Picture for yourself the long-drawn agony of those hours of darkness, in spite of all the hope that fills me, and the senses which are growing dulled; and imagine, if you can, the scene when the night is passing, and the tropic dawn comes quickly.

The daylight shows me dangers which the gloom has mercifully hidden. The mainmast of the sunken *Birkenhead* shoots upwards from the sea, and its spars and rigging are crowded with men, clinging, fly-like, to the ropes and timbers. With bits of mast and wood from the deck, trusses of hay, cabin furniture, and anything and everything that will float, men are holding their heads above water, casting yearning glances towards that shore which is so near and yet so far, and always looking for a sight of sail or help.

What is that strange object which is moving stealthily and swiftly through the water near me? It disappears suddenly, and I know that it is the fin of a shark, which has turned on his back for his savage and always sure attack. There is a piercing cry, and a tinging red of the sea – and the number of survivors is lessened. Time after time that awful drama is played, and the senses are dulled until even such a death is robbed of terror.

Yet even now I cannot help wondering why some are taken and some are left by these monsters of the deep. I do know – and I am thankful for it- that they do not molest me, nor throughout my stay in the water does a shark so much as make a rush at me. They say that the sharks that night and day seized mostly those who were naked, while I had still my greatcoat on, and I keep it on for some time. But it goes at last.

The hours pass slowly, and I am parched with thirst; but I do not let the hope within me die. I am drifting to the land, inch by inch only, because I am held a prisoner in a mass of sea bamboo, which is worse than any weed, and proves the death of many a poor fellow who might escape. It is like a floating jungle. Through this enveloping obstruction I and my spar are driven by the tide towards the coast, and at last I am within a stone's throw of the land.

All this time the men, exhausted, are dropping from the mast into the sea, and are letting go their frail supports; but I am absorbed in my own position, full of my own miseries, able only to thank of my own salvation. I have reached the limit of my endurance, and am the plaything of the sullen swell which rolls ashore.

And now, just when salvation seems assured, I am met by my greatest danger. I am hurled into the heavy surf, which is like to break or crush me. It is as if the ruthless sea was making one last effort to claim me, who have defied it so long, and is determined to wrench me from my spar. But I struggle desperately still, and at last, just after sundown, I am thrown, like flotsam, on the beach, bruised and bleeding, hungry, thirsty, almost senseless, utterly exhausted, and stripped of every scrap of clothing – after eighteen hours in that remorseless sea.

I lie where the waves have thrown me, caring nothing, and fall into a log-like sleep till morning, when I join some of my unhappy comrades who have been saved also.

There – that is my old man's story. What else is there to tell? What else can there be?

I join my regiment, and march and fight as if there had been no *Birkenhead* disaster. It is soldiering – and it is discipline.

Yes, that all-conquering discipline – for of all the women and children not one is lost.

Because of that, and because we obeyed – I and the rest of us are satisfied.

Corporal W. Smith

THE BALTIC FLEET, 1854

Seaman William C. Puxty, RN. *HMS Cressy*

In March 1854, Queen Victoria, in her yacht, led to sea a British Fleet under Sir Charles Napier, to act against Russia in the Baltic during the Crimean War. In conjunction with the French, the fleet bombarded and captured Bomarsund. Afterwards the Gilbraltar of the North, Sweaborg, was attacked; but although the bombardment lasted for two complete days, the Allies failed to subdue it, and the fleets returned home. Early in 1855 a second expedition sailed under Admiral R.S. Dundas; but again the fleets were unsuccessful, and Sweaborg remained unconquered. Mr. W.C. Puxty, who tells this story, served in H.M.S. "Cressy," one of the screw-ships of the line.

I wonder what the gunnery Jack Tars of to-day would think of the infernal machines of the time of the Crimea, and what we, in the Baltic, would have thought if we could have looked ahead for more than half a century, and seen the submarines and destroyers, and the *Dreadnought* and her sister battleship-cruisers? I am too old to know much about the modern improvements in ships and guns, although I do my best to keep in touch with their development; but I am not too far advanced in years to remember the performances of the first infernal machines that were ever used in actual fighting. They were employed against us by the Russians in the Baltic Expedition, and the chief thing about them was that they frequently went off without the slightest warning, and scared us and did tremendous mischief.

Those were still, to a great extent, the days of the sailing ships – the huge wooden structures with their quaint and picturesque figure-heads and long, imposing lines of black and white ports. Even the vessels that had screws were fully rigged, and could carry an enormous press of canvas.

We blockaded the Gulf of Finland in April, 1854, and in July we were joined by about ten thousand French troops, who came out in British ships of war. It was not long before we set to work in grim earnest, and the difficulty we first tackled was the bombardment of the fortress of Bomarsund. This was the first fighting I had seen, and I got intensely excited. Of all the powder monkeys in the fleet – we were the real article in those days – I think I was one of the most active. I had to skip and jump a lot between the magazine and the guns, and keep the sweating, swearing, broiling men supplied with cartridges and ammunition.

My gun was one of the very foremost in the *Cressy,* and I had a long way to go to the magazine, so that whenever we were in action I saw pretty nearly everything that was going on, and saw it clearly, too. I can picture now so vividly the half-naked men at the guns in a smother of choking smoke that caused a dreadful thirst; and can see the tubs of fresh water and baskets of biscuits on the deck near the gun crews. When a man wanted a biscuit or drink he got it – provided the captain of the gun didn't keep him too busily employed in fighting.

Sweaborg, in the Gulf of Finland, was one of the most famous fortresses in the world and was considered then impregnable. The Russians had taken it in 1808. It

The Bombardment of Bomarsund

was built on five rocky islands, the granite fortifications being as solid as the rocks themselves. There were immense quantities of stores and power, mostly in bomb-proof magazines.

Two thousand big guns grinned from the embrasures, guns that were always on a steady platform, while we, on board the ships, were mostly rolling and pitching on the Baltic, firing when we could, and too often missing. Besides the batteries there were Russian ships, which hugged the forts very closely. They had been piloted up the deep channels, through dangerous rocks; but we were not able to get near them, because we had no pilots, and all the buoys and marks had been removed.

In addition to the other precautions further protection was afforded by the presence of a number of infernal machines set afloat in the water by the Russians. These machines were crude and primitive inventions, like a sugar-loaf. The cones were made of galvanised iron, and were about twenty inches long and sixteen in diameter. Each machine held about ten pounds of powder, which was fired by sulphuric acid. I remember them so well because for some time I had to take care of one. It had two tiny things at each side of the top, the nose, so to speak, being downward. I do not quite know what these little things were, but perhaps they were fuses. Anyway, there was also a tiny glass tube in the centre of the machine, and the little fuses were connected with the tube, which a shock would explode.

We had plenty of tedious time on our hands during that long, weary investment of the Northern Gibraltar, and part of it was spent in dragging for mines with grapnels. I saw about thirty brought up. As a rule they were handled very gingerly, because the men were rather afraid of them, being unaccustomed to startling inventions; but occasionally the sailors became reckless in their handling of the freaks.

The *Excellent*, which afterwards became the gunnery ship at Whale Island, Portsmouth, brought up one of the machines with the grapnels. The fearsome thing aroused intense interest, and the crew crowded round to learn something of its secret.

I suppose the machine received an unexpected blow or was suddenly and violently disturbed, for it exploded with a thunderous report, and scattered the clustering group. One officer and two or three men were seriously injured by the accident, which made us all very chary of handling the power-charged cones. They were said to be the invention of a philosopher; but on the whole they did very little damage, although the *Merlin*, a paddle-box war vessel, was partially disabled by the explosion of one over which she passed.

I do not think there was a man in the Allied Fleet, from the Admiral downward, who supposed that the forts could be reduced, much less taken. A modern fleet, I daresay, would find some way of getting at the forts, with the help of steam; but in the Baltic we had to depend largely on canvas, because the screw and paddle steamers were neither fast nor handy. The French had no fewer than seven sailing ships of the line, and only one screw vessel of the same class; while we had thirteen screw steamers of the line, amongst them being the *Cressy*, with her sister ship, the *Majestic*.

Nowadays nothing is left to chance in the Navy, and there does not seem to be any groping in the dark. There is not much in the way of experiment, and I suppose that, if the time comes when the dreadful machines that have been built for fighting purposes have to meet the fleets of an enemy, there will be a battle according to time-table and programme. But in the Baltic manners were in the experimental stage, for the old order of things in the Navy was changing, and the new one had not fully come. There were still serving many of the famous old sea-dogs, and of these the foremost was Sir Charles Napier. All sorts of experiments being made with the object of improving ships and guns, and especially to invent something which would enable us to smash the forts and compel them to surrender.

Many marvellous freaks were brought into existence, but none, I think, was stranger than the two floating batteries, or bombs, which had been sent out from England. One was called the *Hecla*. The lower part was shaped like a boat, and the top of this was a perfectly flat deck or platform, not very big – say about twenty feet or so in diameter. Only one gun was mounted, a muzzle-loading sixty-eight pounder, which was slung from an arrangement of sheers and a derrick, and not mounted in the ordinary way. Each bomb carried about fifty men as a crew.

I was standing on the forecastle head of the *Cressy,* watching the *Hecla,* when I noticed a terrific explosion. In the ordinary way the sixty-eight pounder made noise enough, but this discharge was appalling, and I knew that something uncommon and serious had happened; and so, indeed, it had, for when the smoke had cleared away I saw that the floating battery had been split completely in two, and that the men were struggling in the water. There was some thrilling scenes as the boats of the nearest ships were got out and hurried to the saving of the *Hecla's* crew. They were smart with the boats in those days, and I believe that every man was saved, though a few were pretty badly mangled.

We had plenty of time for brooding in the Baltic, and that was perhaps the cause to some extent of the diseases which attacked us, and from which we suffered heavily.

Go back in naval history and you will find that all the heaviest losses have been caused, not by battle, but by disease. In the old sailing days men were swept off by ship's companies. That did not quite happen in the Baltic; but death came wholesale to us and in one of its most awful forms – cholera. How the disease was brought into my own ship I do not know, but I imagine that it originated with a couple of prisoners, Finns, whom we captured and who were kept on board. Cholera was very bad amongst the Russians, and although these Finns did not personally suffer from the disease they could be the means of spreading it.

As a boy I was not very much disturbed by the pitiful sights I witnessed in the ship – the spectacle of men in the full enjoyment of health and strength being suddenly struck down. Nothing is more demoralising than disease in an army or a fleet, and nothing can be worse than cholera. You know your fate within a few hours. Time after time I saw big, fine fellows buried – men who had been attacked in the most mysterious way. I do not know what the total number of our loss was, but we often had as many as seven or eight funerals a day. It is strange but true, that the finest and strongest men seemed to fall the easiest victims; and it was said in the ship that the heartiest eaters were the worst sufferers and readiest victims.

The boats of the nearest ships were got out and hurried to the saving of the *Hecla's* crew.

But even in those gloomy and tedious days we had our little excitements. One of the liveliest things, I remember, happened at Copenhagen in going out. We were taking in cases of spirits for the captain and the wardroom officers. The cases were hoisted from a lighter alongside, and passed through the lower deck ports, the men standing at certain distances from each other and passing them along aft to the store-room. At the end of the day, when all the cases had been taken from the lighter, it was found that one was missing. Not a trace of it could be discovered. Where was the missing spirit? Had it fallen overboard? Had someone got it? Nobody knew; at any rate nobody would tell. There was checking and re-checking, but all that could be learnt was that the case was missing.

Lights went out at eight o'clock. Two hours afterwards there was a tremendous uproar. I leant out of my hammock and saw that the noise was made by a control of jolly and drunken coastguards. The captain and the master-at-arms hurried up, and after a lot of shuffling and confusion the merrymakers were put in irons on the upper deck. They had their spirits quelled in a very unexpected fashion, for next morning the doctor ordered that the hose should be played on the men – a performance which cooled and sobered them with remarkable swiftness.

Then the mystery of the missing case was solved. The coastguardmen had smuggled it away, and managed to get the bottles into one of the guns. Having done that, they replaced the tompion, and when lights were out they got at the bottles in the darkness and began to make a jolly time of it. The actual thieves were never discovered, if it was really a case of stealing. All that could be proved against the offenders was that they were drunk, and I dare say it was considered that the irons and the hose-pipe were sufficient punishment for the crime.

These coastguardmen were fine fellows, but there was nearly a mutiny against them. In order to man the ships it had been necessary to call the coastguardmen out. In the *Cressy* these men brought their own clothes with them, but our captain was a martinet, and insisted that they should take up "slops," the material from which the crew's clothes generally were made. The coastguardmen grumbled and protested, and proclaimed the right to wear their own clothes, which were smarter and better than the ordinary slops. They felt sore, too, because they had been torn away from their wives and homes.

The captain sent for the Admiral, and Sir Charles came in his famous white waistcoat, discoloured with the snuff which he was always taking. All the hands were mustered – more than a thousand strong – and the Admiral heard the complaint. To the joy of the coastguardmen, he sided with them, and they were not compelled to take up the slops they hated so much. The captain did not like being beaten, but it was better that he should feel sore than that there should be a mutiny.

What happened to the Finns? Well, poor fellows! I am glad to say that they escaped the cholera and lived to go ashore again.

Admiral Napier had a great reputation, and there was an ubounded belief that he would succeed in doing what proved to be impossible. How the general public looked upon his task was shown by some doggerel which was sung at the time, called "Give it to him, Charley!" The poet said:

> I'll tell how British seamen brave
> Of Russian foes will clear the wave,
> Old England's credit for to save,
> Led on by gallant Charley;

and finished by declaring that:

> No Russian foe can e'er withstand
> So brave a man as Charley.

The summer passed and the terrible winter was coming – the bitter cold which would turn the Gulf into a mass of ice and make it impossible for us to remain at sea. Preparations were made to return home, and home we came. And to what? A storm of abuse against the Admiral for having failed to take what proved to be an impregnable fortress – for not having succeeded in doing what all who understood the difficulties in his way knew to be impossible. There were many miserable and bitter quarrels between public men in the days of the Crimea, but there was none more virulent than the troubles which arose concerning Sweaborg.

It was forgotten that the Admiral had been sent away with a fleet which, in many respects, was badly manned – a fleet which did not find itself until a year later, when Admiral Dundas went out with over eighty ships, mounting more than two thousand guns. Sixteen French ships, with more than four hundred guns joined him, making a magnificent and powerful fleet – such a sight as will never be witnessed again. Yet – and is it not wonderful to reflect upon it? – the whole of that vast and stately array could be shattered, if it floated now, by one small, modern cruiser, because she could keep out of the range of their guns, and pound and crush the wooden hulks at her leisure. She could sweep them off the seas, annihilate them, and herself suffer not a scratch.

In August 1855, on the 9th, the Allied Fleets began one of the longest battles that was ever fought at sea. Sweaborg, the unconquered, the impregnable, was to be attacked. Surely a more grandly terrible spectacle was never witnessed than the sight of the enormous Allied Fleets bombarding the forts which we came to know so well and hate so much. Nothing more solemn could be heard or seen than the drums beating to quarters and the men stripping to the waist and taking up their positions at the guns – the old muzzle-loaders of the type with which all England's greatest battles have been won.

The bombardment of Sweaborg was one of the most extraordinary battles ever fought, and one of the longest, for it lasted, practically without a break, for forty-eight hours. Trafalgar, as an actual conflict, began and ended in a few hours, and Waterloo was decided in a short day.

You know how circus horses run round a ring? Well, in the same way the ships of the fleets encompassed the forts at Sweaborg, delivering their fire and making a wonderful battle-ring. The sight iself was marvellous, the terrible-looking forts blazing away on all sides, and the stately ships going round and round with their guns crashing from their yawning ports and the heavy wreaths of powder-smoke hanging low over the water.

For nearly fifty hours the fight went on and the desperate and forlorn attempt was continued. Men who had been white at the start were black with grime and smoke and sweat, and men who had begun in perfect health and strength were utterly exhausted. Yet there was no time to rest, no chance of sleeping; though in some cases nature conquered, and occasionally a gunner would fall at the side of his smoking weapon and snatch a little rest, while there were instances of seamen going about their duties automatically, sleeping as they stood, and serving and working in the sweltering broadside batteries.

The in-battle was not remarkable for casualties, except our freedom from them, for to a large extent we were out of reach of the guns of the fortress. What could be done in such dangerous waters without pilots, and with no buoys or lighthouses to guide us? We had to blaze away and keep pounding, in the hope that we should do some serious mischief; but I think we might almost as well have hammered the distant sky.

During the two long days and nights the furious bombardment continued; then it ceased, because the truth had at last to be recognised that the fortress was unconquerable. The long drawn-out game was up, and our own ships returned, and the French also went away.

The Baltic Expedition had proved a failure, and the Russians were, at any rate, able to say that they had not been beaten on every hand.

We can boast of our Alma, Inkerman, Balaclava, and Sebastopol; Russia can still point with pride to Sweaborg, the unconquered.

THE BURNING OF THE TRANSPORT *SARAH SANDS*, 1857

Private George Diggens, 54th Foot

Our naval annals contain no more thrilling story than the saving of the *Sarah Sands* by the heroic labour and indomitable courage of the 54th Regiment, now the 2nd Battalion, Dorsetshire Regiment. She was an iron screw ship of about 2000 tons, and was taking the troops – 368 in all – from Portsmouth to Calcutta. After leaving the Cape she took fire on November 11th, 1857, and for nearly eighteen hours the after part of her was a roaring furnace. When the fire was mastered, the hulk was sailed to the Mauritius, which was reached without the loss of a single life. Pluck and discipline had saved her. Private George Diggens, whose story is here retold, was the doctor's servant on board, and had exceptional opportunities of seeing what happened. He is now an in-pensioner of Chelsea Hospital.

We were going out to India to help quell the Mutiny, nearly fifty years ago. And we were going in the *Sarah Sands*, whose voyage was to be one of the most disastrous that any ship has survived.

For two long, dreary months, the *Sarah Sands* slowly forced her way south; then we reached the Cape, and after being there a week, coaling, we set out again for Calcutta. The voyage had not been without incident of a sort – the sort you would rather be without. For one thing, death came unexpectedly in our midst, and threw a shadow on the ship. There was a fine, high-spirited man amongst the crew – Dutchman, I think – who was the very life of us. He was always cheerful, always full of sport, which he worked off in merrymaking. One day he was skylarking, when he suddenly fell overboard. Strangely enough, we never saw a sign of him, except his cap, which came to the surface. But we were in the tropics then, and sharks swarmed about the transport. We had a good deal to do with these monsters of the sea before our woes were ended.

Another thing which troubled us was the crew. You must remember that in those days, when so many ships were wanted to take troops to India, any sort of human being who called himself a sailor was certain of employment. British seamen were scarce, and our commander, Captain Castle – he died about a year ago – was forced to ship a miscellaneous lot. They were nearly all foreigners and mutinous scoundrels. This being the case, is it necessary to say that they were also cowards?

Well, there you have a picture of us – about 500 souls, all told, in a small screw steamboat – a mutinous crew, taking our troops to crush a mutiny! Such we were when we left the Cape to make our way past Ceylon, and up the Indian Ocean and the Bay of Bengal to Calcutta.

Bad as the first part of the voyage had been, the second was infinitely worse. It seemed as if a curse settled on the vessel from the very outset. Some of the mutineers were in irons, and had been kept on bread and water for seven days. It has been said – and I, for one, do not disbelieve it – that the mutineers even went so far as to cause the mysterious fire which nearly brought about the destruction of us all.

We were heavy laden when we left the Cape, deep with the coal and fresh water and stores we had taken on board. We drove into bad weather, too, and on November 7th a squall considerably damaged us. But these disasters were trifles in comparison with the great calamity which they preceded.

We were about a thousand miles away from the Cape, alone on the sea. We had had our dinner, and the officers and ladies were just ready for theirs. It was about half-past two – they dined early in the Fifties, especially on board ship – and we were smoking our pipes and sitting about chatting and laughing, and passing the time pleasantly enough, as shipboard life went.

I was rather a favoured person, because, as servant to Dr. O'Donovan, I was allowed an extra pint of porter daily. I went below to get my drink, and was instantly met by an awful smell of burning. I knew too well the terrible danger we were in if fire broke out to lose a minute's time in making known what I had seen. I returned to the deck, and just on reaching the top of the hatchway, I met the carpenter. "I believe the ship's on fire!" I told him.

"Sh!" he answered. "You'll be put in irons if you say that!"

But he hurried below and hurried back again, and almost instantly Captain Castle and the chief mate came along.

There was no need to mince matters then, or hide the awful truth. The *Sarah Sands* was burning, and every soul on board knew it. The hatches were closed down, so that no unnecessary draught should feed the fire, but it was soon too clear that the transport was a roaring blaze astern.

Without the slightest warning we had been plunged from peace and safety into tumult and peril. We were fighting a battle in which the odds were crushingly against us. Now came the test of courage and endurance, and proof again, if proof were needed, of the steadying power of discipline. What of the mutineers, the foreigners, who knew neither drill or obedience, and who had no *esprit de corps* to hold them to their duty? They had rushed to the boats and jumped into them, and caring nothing for anything except their own skins, had pushed off.

A few of the 54th, who, in the confusion, had jumped into the boats also, were carried away from the ship's side. It had been just possible to get the ladies and children into one of the boats, and in it, covered with blankets and anything else we could lay hands on in the hurry and excitement, they were huddled during those long, awful hours of daylight and darkness in which we struggled to beat the flames and save the ship. Their case was as melancholy as our own, for the weather was proving bad, and the boats were thrown about by the seas – one, indeed, was swamped, but no lives were lost. Fortunately, as we were going on active service, there were very few women and children on board – eleven in all.

When the fire broke out, the *Sarah Sands* was carrying sail. The commander ordered this to be taken in, and also that the ship should be got, and kept, head to wind. That was, of course, to try to keep the fire from extending, by confining it to the after part of the transport. This was a hard enough task with so few sailors left on board; but during the long voyage some of us had picked up a little seamanship, and so, under the direction and with the help of the ship's officers, we managed it. Hose-pipes were fitted to the fire-engine, buckets and anything from which water could be thrown were furiously at work. We did everything that mortal men could do to drown the flames, and yet our puny jets had not the least effect on them.

Merciful indeed it is that at such times great exertions keep us from dwelling overmuch on what may seem our hopeless case. If there had been a chance for thought, for calculating the overwhelming odds against us, there were not many even of the bravest but would have resignedly awaited the end, and prayed for its speedy coming; but every nerve and every muscle in every man was alert and working, and like very fiends the 54th laboured for the preservation of the *Sarah Sands*.

Even at a time of the greatest peril some unexpected incident will force us to the thought of matters other than our personal doings. Here were we, overshadowed by present horrors, and the prospect of an almost certain death; yet there arose a strange forgetfulness of self and a concern for the welfare of a fellow-creature. And who was he? Where was he that he should claim attention then, of all times? Where could he have been for his case to be worse than our own pitiful plight?

He was a prisoner below, a mutineer in irons, and he was captive in the heart of that fiery furnace!

This seemed the very crowning horror of our case. He was a sailor – a one-eyed man, called Scottie, the best of the crew; and there he was helpless below. Instantly there were men willing to risk their lives to try to save him; but no man was allowed to make the attempt; all that we were permitted to do was to throw a rope down in the feeble hope that he could help himself. A rope was lowered, and Scottie managed to seize it. Then we dragged him up to the deck, irons and all, and he got his poor chance of life like the rest of us. But there were few who thought he could pull round, for he was too overcome with exhaustion that he lay on the deck like one dead, and it was fully twenty minutes before he recovered consciousness.

First and foremost to the soldier of the old days came the thought of his regimental Colours. Ours were in the saloon, and the saloon was astern, where the fire was raging. Who would venture on such a forlorn hope as the attempt to save them? Who, indeed? Why, there was an instant dash for them, without thought of personal danger, in defiance of the stifling smoke and scorching flames. First of all, the two ensigns into whose special care the Colours had been given – Lieutenants Houston and Hughes – rushed into the choking saloon and tried to seize the precious folds of silk and bring them out. They failed, and barely escaped with their lives.

Then a gallant fellow named Richard Richmond, one of the ship's quartermasters, vanished into the dense smoke and struggled towards the far end of the saloon, where the Colours hung. He had a wet cloth over his face, and was armed with an axe. With frantic cuts he got the Colours down and staggered back through the suffocating atmosphere. Then, overcome with the heat and smoke, he fainted, and it seemed as if his death were as sure as the destruction of the Colours and ship.

But pluck begets pluck. There was another rush, and Private William Wiles dragged Richmond and the Colours from the saloon and on to the deck. They came out of that awful furnace with just strength enough to hold the Colours up so that the 54th should see them, and in that thrilling act and with our cheers ringing in their ears, they fell down senseless and exhausted. These Colours are now in Norwich Cathedral.

We were in the very thick of our fight, whetted to continue it by the salvation of our Colours, and the ceaseless encouragement and glorious example of our regimental officers. Their pluck was as wonderful as their endurance. And they were finely supported by the ship's officers and the two or three men – Englishmen, mind you – of the crew who had not deserted to the boats. Courage and an unfaltering lead were needed, too, for we had no human enemy to deal with, no opposing troops who at any moment might break and run; but a grim and ruthless foe who had it all his own way, and with whom the very wind and sea appeared to be in league, for the wind was roaring and the waves were running high.

We were formed in sections – drill, drill, drill, it seemed to be on that rolling, burning parade-ground – and a curious sight we must have been, because we were always counter-marching. We were crowded on the cramped fore part of the ship, and were always facing ourselves, so to speak. That was owing to some of us coming up from below, where we had been sent to work, and marching forward and meeting the sections who were on their way to relieve us.

It seems easy to talk about pouring water on the fire, but no tongue can tell the difficulties we had to meet and overcome. Before we could get below we had to cut holes in the deck with hatchets; then to grope and stifle in the dense, hot depths, feeling with our hands for the hottest places on the iron plates, and throwing water on to keep them cool. A ceaseless wetting of the coals was also necesary to keep them from bursting into flames.

We crawled and crept and staggered blindly from spot to spot with our buckets and other things, always to keep the fire to its huge metal grate and prevent it from bursting out into the whole of our home. We never stopped throwing the water down, and never ceased to pump it up again, so that the *Sarah Sands* should not meet her doom from her only means of preservation.

Now that we were accustomed to the first great danger, we were confronted with another and more awful peril, and that was our destruction by the explosion of the powder in our two magazines. We had many barrels of gunpowder on board, and, in addition, there was the ship's rockets in another magazine. Not even the bravest could think of that new peril without fear; but the terror disappeared in the fury and excitement of getting at the casks.

First to be tackled was the starboard magazine, and the 54th fell to their work with all the strength that dread gives – almost, if you like, despairingly. The task was so hard, the means of doing it so slight. Everything was against us, and it seemed as if nothing were in our favour. To get at the powder meant that the men had to be lowered with ropes through the holes in the deck into the suffocating, scorching depths, and to fasten other ropes round casks, when these were hauled up. Each cask as it was landed on the deck was thrown overboard. One by one they came, men working until they could work no more – some indeed were drawn up senseless – and at last the starboard magazine was emptied.

Again there was a thrill of triumph, but short-lived, for the port quarter magazine was still untouched, and it was very near the fire. It could be reached only by one hatchway, and that was already belching dense clouds of hot smoke.

Volunteers were wanted again – volunteers were instantly at hand.

The furious fight to get the powder overboard was renewed. Again men went below and laboured until they fainted; but the powder diminished and grew less, until at last there remained only one cask of ammunition which an exhausted soldier had dropped, and some signalling powder which had been forgotten. There were also two large barrels of powder which it was humanely possible to reach.

Our fate seemed sure at last.

We had so far escaped the fire and kept it to the stern; the ship was still manageable, and might be saved, but the powder was certain to explode, and there was no one who believed that the *Sarah Sands* would survive the explosion. We had been striving for hours, darkness had settled on the sea, and it seemed as if nothing could be done. The boats – can you imagine the feelings of the unhappy women and children in them, separated from husbands and fathers, tossed on the waters, and expecting certain death? – were ordered to get clear of the ship so as to escape the force of the explosion, and they were pulled away.

No one can indicate the sufferings of those who waited in the boats and in the ship for the awful end – agonies which were intensified by the enforced partings.

Again desperate exertions kept us employed. We never ceased to try to save the ship. We cut away the deck fittings which might catch fire, and cabins and lumber went overboard; we collected the spars and other things and made three rafts. Two of these were set afloat and the third was left across the deck, ready to be lowered at the very last.

To the glory of the 54th be it said that not even then, in the very face of death, with the conviction that the ship might at any moment explode, did a single soldier rush for the rafts. The troops remained obedient, and the officers continued to encourage and lead them.

It was about this time that Captain Castle, brave though he was, abandoned hope. He was on the bridge – I was there also, with the doctor – and turning to Major Brett, who was in command of us, he said, "You have done all you can; nothing more is possible." Then he took a pair of marine glasses which were slung over his shoulders, and flung them into the heart of the fire saying, "They're no good now!" But Major Brett answered,

"We shall never stop working till we're driven overboard."

In the darkness of the night the flames leapt skyward. The after part of the ship was by that time one mass of fire. The deck was burnt away, the iron beams were red hot, the very sides were glowing, and to the roaring of the fire and wind and sea there was the appalling accompaniment of an unearthly light for miles around – a vaporous and unnatural luminosity. The sky itself was a vast red dome, and the very sea was ghastly with the glare.

Most horrible of all, the water swarmed with sharks, which were quite clearly visible as they leapt and struggled, hungrily waiting for the end.

Would the end never come? Would this nerve-destroying suspense never be broken? Would the fire never reach the powder?

Can you picture the pitiful sight of us – the troops still fighting, as we were fighting, against these overwhelming odds of fire and wind and sea? Could there be no mercy of any sort for us?

Even as we watched and waited and hoped the tarred mizzen rigging took fire. The ropes swiftly burnt away and over crashed the mast. Still, in the good providence of God, and because we plied our work with hose and bucket, we kept the *Sarah Sands* head to wind, and so preserved her, keeping the fire confined to the after part, although once or twice terrible blasts of flame and smoke were swept from stern to bow.

We had been striving for many long hours. Man after man had fallen senseless, dropping exhausted on the deck, and the only thing even the doctor could do was to throw salt water on their faces to bring them around. Our uniforms were scorched from our bodies, our skins were burnt and black with smoke, and we were parched with torturing thirst. Believe me, so terrible was this thirst upon us that our tongues were swollen out of our mouths, and could be forced back only by the pressure of our hands. And there was no relief for us, because our very life's sustenance, our food and drink, were being destroyed with our ship.

Suddenly there was the terrifying climax for which we had all been waiting.

Right astern there was a mighty red flash upward, a deafening crash, a crackling as if the very elements were dissolving, then a shuddering, sickening sinking of our waterladen troopship.

The powder had exploded at last, and with it had burst the ship's rockets, making such a firework show as never mortal man had seen, I think, for he had never witnessed it in such a setting – and such a one as I have no desire to look upon again.

Not a human being in the transport who felt the shock, not a wretched soul in the boats who saw the awful sight, believed that the vessel would survive, and yet when the shudder had passed through her, when she had recovered from that sickening dip, the *Sarah Sands* rode still, although the wreckage of her stern cabins had been blown out and into fragments and a great hole torn in her port quarter as far down as the water-line. Marvellous to tell, the explosion injured only two amongst us, a lieutenant and a corporal, who were blown down a hatchway, but were rescued.

We were still afloat, then – still favoured with a dismal hope of preservation. And so we went into the fight again with fresh heart of grace, and the buckets were passed and the hoses played, and on to the hot coal and the heated plates of her we threw the water, in the hope that even yet we might prevent the fire from spreading, as for many hours, thank God, we had prevented it.

Throughout that unspeakable night the 54th fought on, unaided by the cowards who had mutinied and left the ship. They were hailed to come and take the *Sarah Sands* in tow, in order to keep her head to the wind, but they refused, and it was not until all danger from the fire was over that they came on board again. They got a reception which made their ears tingle, I can assure you. The sharks had tried repeatedly to upset the boats with their tails, and now that they saw the people returning to the ship they made savage and voracious rushes at them. More than one nigger's face went white than if it had been washed as the huge jaws snapped near him.

I have seen pictures of fine people going back to burnt-out homes. So it was with the *Sarah Sands*. Her beautifully dressed women, who had been hurried into the boats with bare arms and necks and shoulders, came to the side again. But how different from the joyous, chatty crowd who were on the point of dining when the cry of "Fire!" was raised! Dresses were torn and crumpled, happy faces had become drawn and haggard, bright eyes were dull with weeping, and white, delicate skins were browned and blistered by the merciless tropical sun. They filled with pity even those of us who had fought the flames, and in looking on their miseries we forgot our own. Captain Castle did what he could to relieve them, and that was to order the sailmaker to get pieces of sail and canvas and make such coverings as he could for the scorched skins. And so upon the delicate finery was put a coarse canvas crown! There was no chance of luxury in such a floating shell, and all that ingenuity could do and provide was to rig a canvas screen to separate the ladies from the troops.

It is astonishing to think what men can reconcile themselves to when they are the creatures of crippling circumstances. Here were we, who had been so cooped up in a small ship on a long run to India, that we could scarcely move in our narrow quarters and close imprisonment; yet we were finding it possible to exist in half the space, huddled almost indiscriminately in an iron shell that only kept afloat by a miracle.

The after part of the transport was just a gutted mass of ironwork, open to the air and sea. To look down into it was like being on the top of a building that has been destroyed by fire, with only bare girders and the gaunt walls visible. The cabins had been blown out of the stern by the explosion; all the woodwork had long since vanished, and some of the iron had melted away. How could it be otherwise with a heat which was so fierce that the very glass of the scuttles had melted and hung like icicles now that it was cold? That fact alone will show you how intense was the heat – literally a furnace heat. It is marvellous that the work of man could withstand a consuming flame, and the survival of the ship was a noble tribute to the stoutness of her structure and the honesty of her build. She had been gutted by fire; now heavy seas struck her repeatedly, and as she rolled helplessly our four enormous tanks of water, which were right below, were hurled from side to side, and we never knew when one or all of them would dash through the iron plating.

Strange and incongruous were the things we did after and resulting from the fire. Most striking of all, I think, was the erection of a tent – for the captain's use and other official purposes – on the iron wreckage, where the stern cabins had been.

A tent on a floating wreck, in that wilderness of tropical sea!
And below that tent was the torn, bent mass of ironwork, with the very propeller-shaft showing in the depths. Need a man be a sailor to understand our constant peril from shipping a sea, or even a mass of water which, in ordinary times, would only cause amusement?

The long fight was over and a glorious victory was won. But what was our price? A mere hull, a ship half burnt away, and which was sound only forward of the mainmast.

The smoke had gone and now only clouds of steam ascended and vanished in the air. The *Sarah Sands* had nearly twenty feet of water in her, and was so deep by the stern that every wave seemed as if it would overwhelm and sink her. We had only one sound mast, too, the mizzen having been burnt away and the main damaged.

We had saved the troopship from fire; now we had to preserve her from water so we set to work again and patched her up. For a long time she was like a gigantic kettle aft, with the steam rising from her, but we pumped incessantly for two nights and a day; we rigged up a steering-gear, we covered over the rent side with spars and canvas, and we got some sail up. That was after foundering and drifting helplessly about in a ship that had nothing to control her.

Then, suffering torture from thirst and hunger, because our fresh water and our provisions had been almost entirely destroyed, we struggled on for nine days more, when we got our gallant cripple into Port Louis in the Mauritius. Until that time from the hour we started from the Cape we had seen neither ship nor land, so our deliverance was merciful indeed. If we had vanished, our fate would never have been known, because two or three bottles that were thrown overboard with messages were never picked up.

The irony of our fate was on us to the very last. A pilot came off and told us that he cuold not take us in till next morning, as ships were not allowed to enter in the darkness. No exception was even made for us, so for the first time since the fire the crazy screw was started slowly, and the *Sarah Sands* crawled off and on. She was nearly wrecked in the night on a reef, but in the morning she got in and we went ashore – some of us wrapped in newspapers to hide our nakedness.

For all the miseries we had suffered there was almost recompense in the things that were said about us, and the kindness which was shown. We had gone through that long-drawn time of peril from fire and sea and mutiny; we had saved our Colours and our ship; we had held to our discipline and maintained the credit of our regiment, and we had not lost a life!

Can you wonder that of all the honours which the 54th has gained there is none it holds dearer than this great triumph that was won upon the sea, and not the battlefield?

THE FIRST IRONCLAD FIGHT: THE *MERRIMAC* AND THE *MONITOR,* 1862

Corporal John Kerrigan, Ellesworth's Fire Souaves

The famous fight between the Confederate iron-plated ship *Merrimac* and the Federal ironclad floating battery *Monitor,* during the American Civil War, proved the most important event in modern naval history. The combat sealed the fate of the old sailing ships, and began the amazing era of the armoured vessel. In Hampton Roads, off the coast of Virginia, on March 8th, 1862, the *Merrimac* destroyed the Federal sailing ships *Cumberland* and *Congress;* but next day the *Monitor* unexpectedly appeared, and repulsed her. Mr. John Kerrigan, who tells the story of the first ironclad fight in history, is a veteran of the Civil War, and other campaigns. He was corporal of C Company of the 11th Regiment of New York Volunteer Infantry, known as Ellesworth's Fire Zouaves. He resides in New York, where most of his life has been spent.

I was quartered in the Water Battery at Fortress Monroe, which overlooked Hampton Roads, and in Hampton Roads, early in 1862, I saw some of the last of the old wooden walls.

The Civil War was raging fiercely. There had been plenty of fighting both by land and sea; but the battles had been just what you would have expected, especially on the water, where the old order of things reigned. Everybody knew that inventors were hard at work evolving some type of ironclad. You in England had built the *Warrior.* We in America were producing the *Merrimac* and the *Monitor.* Ironclads had come into existence, but there was nothing so far to show what they could do in action, because they had not been put to the test.

I was neither looking for nor expecting that event which revolutionised naval warfare. I gazed from the fort across the Roads, where some of the finest specimens of wooden ships afloat were riding peacefully at anchor. They were the frigates *Cumberland, Congress, Roanoake,* and *Minnesota.* A few smaller vessels were about, but I will not trouble with them. I want to continue my story almost exclusively to the fight between the first famous ironclads.

The *Cumberland* was a very fine sailing ship, and her men were never tired of talking, when they came ashore, of what she was and what she could do. They declared that she was more than a match for anything that the other side could put up against her. The men of the *Congress* bragged too, saying that their ship had the biggest-calibred guns afloat. The weapons were certainly very formidable.

The ships were anchored in the Roads, very near the Water Battery, which ran right down to the beach, and on that fine spring morning, finer because it succeeded a night of storm, they looked just as if no such dreadful thing as war existed.

Then, abruptly, a little after midday, I heard the drums beat to quarters, and saw the two thousand officers and men who manned the ships prepare for action, for the *Merrimac* had been bearing down upon them. We in the Water Battery stood to our guns and rifles.

The *Merrimac* was a very strange ship. She was originally a steam frigate, and had been sunk and set on fire so that she should not fall into the hands of the enemy – the Southerners. But the Southerners had raised her, and most ingeniously turned her into a crude ironclad, using railway rails as armour. An iron prow was put on to her, and on the deck, which had been cut down to something like two feet above the waterline, they fitted the rails as iron plates, just after the style of the roof of a house.

The *Merrimac* looked an extraordinary object as she came into sight, and she caused just the same flutter of fear that you might expect among a flock of sheep when a strong, unknown enemy appears. There had been plenty of scoffing at the converted frigate, but we all distrust the unknown, and the *Merrimac* was a dreadful kind of mystery. She looked so grim and business-like, such possiblities seemed to be hidden in her sloping sides, and her guns, not many of them, but very powerful for those days, gave such promise to mischief amongst the hulls and spars of the anchored ships. They presented so much to blaze away at; while the *Merrimac* was comparatively nothing of a target.

I do not suppose that naval history offers an instance of swifter and more terrific carnage than the fight which came upon us like a bolt from the blue.

Just as some awful monster might have swooped on its helpless prey, so that *Merrimac* headed towards the anchored wooden ships, not even a single person being visible on her deck.

I watched her uncanny bulk making for the *Congress;* then from her iron sides I saw the fierce, red flashes of the big guns, and heard the boom of the broadside which she had sent crashing into the *Congress.* There was the answering thunder of the wooden frigate's broadside; but she might as well have trained her vaunted guns skyward. The shot rattled harmlessly, like peas, upon the sloping hull of the *Merrimac,* and scattered without doing any mischief; while the ironclad's fire showed instantly that the battle was hers, to fight as she liked. She had only to take her time, and pick the anchored ships off one by one. Her opening broadside was a mere whetting of her appetite, and when she had discharged it she began, with murderous deliberation, to steam across the *Cumberland's* bows, with the object of prowing her – ramming, you call it.

But the time for ramming had not come. The *Merrimac,* which steamed and steered badly, could not manage that at the very beginning of things. She could, however, use her guns, and she did so with terrible effect. She sent in a shot which, so we learnt afterwards, killed and wounded nearly a dozen marines, and after that, for something like twenty minutes, the ironclad did as she pleased with her prey. She beat and battered her, just as some powerful combatant might punish a helpless adversary.

Every shot from the *Merrimac* told. The *Cumberland's* crew were being slain, and the ship herself was being so badly damaged that she was sinking at her anchor. I saw the fatal effect of the ironclad's shot, and observed that every ball whch struck the *Merrimac* flew off the sloping hull, skipping up in the air, and producing no effect whatsoever. Even above the roar of the fight I could hear the cries of the wounded and the fierce shouts of the officers and men of the *Cumberland.* We knew afterwards how terrible the carnage in the *Cumberland* had been; and I saw even while the fight was raging that the dead were being thrown overboard. I did not need to be told what it

The *Cumberland* was doomed . . . and the water was surging in through her shattered ports and gaping sides.

meant below, in the reeking, smoking deck-spaces, where the dead had to lie where they fell under the pitiless hail of the *Merrimac's* fire.

The *Cumberland* was doomed. That was certain, and none knew better than her own people that she could not keep afloat. Her decks were red and slippery with blood, her timbers were beaten in, and the water was surging through her shattered ports and gaping sides. She was settling by the head – an awesome but inspiring spectacle; yet she fought on with the most amazing courage.

The captain of the *Merrimac* was called Buchanan, and I distinctly heard him shout: "Do you surrender?"

"No! Sink us first!" the captain of the *Cumberland* shouted back.

No more was said. War is war, and knows no mercy.

Again the *Merrimac* discharged a broadside, and her terrible shot finished the havoc of her cannonade. But even yet she had not done her work; she had not used that weapon which experience has shown to be more fatal than the guns themselves, and that is the ram. Was not your own superb *Victoria* sent to the bottom of the Mediterranean by the ram of the *Camperdown?*

The *Merrimac* headed for the *Cumberland,* and prowed her just below the waterline. Then, head first, with her flag still flying, the *Cumberland* sank in the water where, so lately, she had floated so proudly. Many brave souls went with her. For more than two months her flag was flying from her masthead.

Whilst this fierce and hopeless fight was being waged by the *Cumberland,* the *Congress* was striving furiously to escape, seeing how impossible it was for wooden ships to hold out against the ironclad. She had slipped her cable and crowded on all sail, so that she could run ashore and avoid capture. She came to within about five hundred yards of our battery; but the *Merrimac* was quickly after her, and at a very short range battered her terribly with her guns. If the *Congress* had been in deep water she would most surely have shared the fate of the *Cumberland,* because it was utterly impossible for her to make any stand against the new engine of war that had so unexpectedly swooped upon the anchored ships.

Time after time it seemed as if the *Congress* were set on by the *Merrimac's* cannonade. She stubbornly refused to surrender, even with the awful and fatal example of the *Cumberland* before her; but when it was seen that it would be nothing short of foolish self-sacrifice to continue the conflict against such overwhelming odds, the flag was hauled down in token of surrender. Some of the officers and men were taken prisoners by a small steamer that came up; but others got ashore by means of boats which we launched from Fortress Monroe. There was no hope of saving the *Congress,* and I watched her as the flames reached her shotted guns and fired them. Then, late that dreadful night, there was a thunderous report, and the *Congress* was shattered into fragments. The magazine itself, containing tons of gunpowder had exploded.

The *Merrimac* steamed away triumphantly, having done the most mischief in the shortest time, I think, that any ship of war ever accomplished.

I myself, who had seen her come and watched her at her awful work, could not realise what had happened. I could not believe that the fine and powerful ships of war which had been so proudly riding at their anchors were destroyed, and that so many of the officers and men who had boasted of their invincibility were slain or drowned. But they had at any rate died gloriously. I needed nothing more than a glance towards the masthead of the *Cumberland* to be reminded of that.

We were a gloomy and disheartened company in Fortress Monroe on the day of our defeat and what looked like downfall. Nothing seemed easier than that the *Merrimac* should come back and destroy our ships of war at her leisure; and nothing was more likely that than she would set to work at once and do it. She had made such a marvellously successful start, and why should she not have an equally victorious finish?

Often enough, when the skies seem darkest, there comes the brightest shafts of light – perhaps they are brighter because of contrast with the gloom; and even before that melancholy Saturday was ended the hope of triumph was born within us.

Both sides in that pitiless and dreadful war had been ceaselessly busy, trying to evolve some new form of fighting ship. The *Merrimac* had been created and sent against us; but we had not been sleeping nor idle, for Captain Ericsson, a Swede, had produced a fighting machine which was even more of a freak than the *Merrimac*. This was the *Monitor*, mother of turret ships, and the model on which, later, your own British warships, the *Thunderer, Dreadnought,* and *Devastation* were built.

The night fell and the darkness crowned the gloom of our spirits. But in the morning there was awaiting the *Merrimac* a suprise and a shock which were equal to anything she had given to her opponents.

During the night the *Merrimac* had been hovering around, waiting for the dawn to come, so that she could renew and finish her dreadful work, and attack the Water Battery as well as the ships.

In the night, however, the *Monitor* had appeared – a ship of war that looked exactly like a raft, with an enormous cheese-box stuck on it. She was really a floating round fort, the turret being of great size; but it differed from a land fort in this way - it revolved by steam power. The *Monitor* herself was heavily armoured, and the inventor had provided her with all sorts of devices which are common enough in these days of skill and science, but were reckoned wonders then.

Picture, if you can, the intense excitement of everyone afloat and ashore at Hampton Roads, when it was seen that a battle was to be fought which would perhaps mean the destruction of the ship that had done so much damage and caused such a heavy loss of life.

There was on our own part a fierce desire for vengeance.

Great crowds of spectators had watched the fight before, and now they reassembled, climbing up rigging and roofs of houses, and swarming on the beach. My own fort was on a shelving bank, running up the shore, the ground behind it being a sort of bluff or cliff. On this bluff the whole of the regiments that were attached to the brigade were drawn up. During the fight between the *Merrimac* and the wooden ships I had seen the shot fly furiously, and I expected now that I should look upon a far more thrilling and terrific combat.

I was not wrong in my assumption. I watched the two strange fighters get closer and closer together, stealing stealthily towards each other, half distrustful, half afraid. They were grotesque, yet awful, and one of them at least had shown her dreadful power as a destroyer of ships and men.

What would the turret ship do? How would the uncanny but apparently formidable cheese-box on a raft come out of the fray, the beginning of which was awaited so breathlessly?

It was awe-inspiring to see the two armoured monsters approaching one another on that silent Sunday morning in Hampton Road. They got nearer and nearer, then, when a very short distance separated them, there were flashes of both, and dull crashes as the reports of the big guns reached my ears.

The battle of the ironclads had begun; but at the outset no impression was made by the cannon. There was no sign of life on the deck of either ship.

Seafighters were incased in iron for the first time in naval warfare, and it was strange and solemn to watch the two steamers, like grim, weird creatures of the waves, gradually get nearer together, spitting savagely with their guns, but still doing no mischief. Then, just as two fierce animals will rush and meet when they have been growling and snarling, the *Merrimac* and the *Monitor* began their real contest.

They got within a few yards of each other, and guns boomed as fast as they could be loaded and discharged. The *Merrimac* had ten weapons, while the *Monitor* carried only two, but the pair were very heavy cannon for those days, and could be run in for loading. When they were quite in the turret the ports were protected by thick slabs of metal which filled the opening. The guns had this advantage, too, that they could be revolved and brought on to bear on the *Merrimac*, no matter how the head of the *Monitor* pointed, whereas the guns of the *Merrimac* could be worked only within a certain radius.

The *Merrimac* had been damaged in her earlier fight, one side of her having been struck, as far as I could see, by some of the shot of the *Cumberland*. It was upon this wounded spot that the *Monitor* directed her terrific fire. She wanted to smash the *Merrimac* as the *Merrimac* had smashed the wooden ships, and so she steamed and dodged about to get what, in the earlier sailing days, would have been the weather gauge.

I watched the two ships circling around each other. Quite half-a-dozen times the *Monitor* steamed round her opponent, and the roar of her big guns, at what seemed like long intervals, was answered by the more frequent crashes of the broadside of the *Merrimac*. If even a fraction of the fire that each ship discharged had been brought to bear on the wooden walls that were not far away, the stout old timbers would have been shattered like matchwood, just as the hull of the *Cumberland* had been smashed.

It was the purpose of the *Monitor* to pour her fire into the hole which had been made in the side of the *Merrimac*, and the object of the latter to protect the weakest part of her.

The fight, fair and equal, went on without a break, the guns flashing and crashing, and the two steamers skirting round and about each other in a welter of smoke and flame. Shot flew over the Water Battery, it thudded against the sloping sides of the

Merrimac, and was sent by her in return towards the huge, cheese-like structure on the raft; yet amazingly little mischief was done.

Meanwhile I was watching, spellbound, cheering wildly when I thought that the *Monitor* had scored, and holding my breath tensely when it seemed as if the *Merrimac* would win. There came the time when the *Merrimac* tried her deadly ram again; but the *Monitor* saw her purpose. She was the faster steamer, too, and slipped out of the way in time to save herself.

Then the *Merrimac* really struck the *Monitor,* and instantly her people boarded the raft-like ship. But there was nowhere to rush, there were no men to kill; more than that, the terrible turret revolved, and not even the victors of the day before cared to stand their ground and be blown to atoms. They got back to the *Merrimac* just as fast as they had rushed upon the deck of the *Monitor.*

For about five hours this unprecedented fight went on. Long before the first hour was ended the *Merrimac* knew that she had caught a Tartar, and that she would be lucky if she got away with a whole skin. She could make no impression on the cheese-box, and as for the raft, she might as well have bombarded the heavens for all the damage she did. Just as the shot of the wooden ships had rattled off her own sloping, roof-like upper works, so her big missiles glanced from the turret's rounded iron sides.

Matters were becoming desperate. The *Merrimac's* people saw, I think, that they would never win with gunnery, and they turned again to the ram whose cruel power they had so completely proved.

The *Merrimac* surged towards the *Monitor,* and it looked as if the latter's doom were certain; but in spite of her unpromising and uncanny appearance she was a handy ship, and steamed and steered well. She slipped out of the way of the *Merrimac,* but the opposing ironclad bore down again upon her and this time she actually did strike her nearly amidships.

I held my breath again, and as the *Merrimac* backed out I expected to see the *Monitor* disappear. Instead of doing that, however, the floating cheese-box plumped one of her enormous shots straight into the *Merrimac.*

That, I think, was really the beginning of the end of the battle. The *Merrimac* realised at last, after a game, stern fight, that she had met her match, or more, and the people of the *Monitor* began to pound her at their leisure. They economised their shot, and the big guns were fired more slowly: but every missile told now, and then, one after the other it seemed, the *Merrimac* received two or three shots which entered the very vitals of her. A few more like them, and she would be forced to surrender or to sink.

The *Merrimac* now saw that she was beaten, and made the best of it. She began to steam as hard as she could – but not towards the *Monitor.* She hurried off at top speed, leaving her opponent victorious, if you can call it triumph, for the *Monitor* was content to remain where she was without giving chase.

During these two fights I had been watching from the Water Battery, regardless of the shots that fell about us. They went far inland, too, and a shell killed a negro who was a mile away from the shore. The shells struck the enbankment near the battery

Then the *Merrimac* really struck the *Monitor*, and instantly her people boarded the raft-like ship.

and exploded there, making such enormous holes in the sandy ground that you could easily have driven a coal cart into them. We ourselves had a splendid gun, a Columbaid it was called – a smooth-bore cannon which was considered one of the finest in the service – and we fired that at the *Merrimac* when we got the chance.

The ironclads had met and fought, and they had taught the whole world the startling lesson that naval warfare was revolutionised. Everybody was thrown into feverish excitement, not knowing what a day would bring forth in the way of inventions. The *Merrimac* had withdrawn to Norfolk.

In the meantime the people at Fortress Monroe and the United States Government had accepted the *Commodore Vanderbill,* a ship of five or six thousand tons, and set to work to turn her into a ram. Her bow, for a distance of fifty or sixty feet, was bagged with cotton bales, in order to resist the effect of any of the *Merrimac's* guns; but her great object was to ram the *Merrimac* and sink her, if she got the chance. This was told to me by several of the crew who shipped on board of her. It was to be a very dangerous business and they knew it. So did the authorities, who induced the men to enlist for the work by giving them three months' pay in advance.

The *Merrimac* had been out of sight for something like ten days when she reappeared and passed our vessels, amongst them being the *Monitor,* and some other strange new ironclads, which had been brought up. Amongst these was a floating battery called the *Nancy Stevens,* which had only one gun, and another ironclad named the *Ironside.* The *Merrimac* steamed up, then, without firing a shot, she turned and went away, nor did our own ships seek to bring her to action. I really think that just for the time being both sides had had enough of it. The *Monitor* had been so severely mauled and strained in her contest with the *Merrimac* that it was not long before she foundered.

I thought that I had seen the last of the *Merrimac.* At least I hoped so; but her end was not due just then. Some weeks afterwards, however, I and other men were thrown out of our bunks by a loud and terrible explosion.

I rushed into the open air and looked towards Norfolk.

I saw an immense column of fire and sparks, remaining in the air like a gigantic pillar.

I gazed, spellbound, wondering what it meant and asking those around me if they knew. But they were as ignorant of the cause as I was.

Next morning I was told that the Confederates had blown up the *Merrimac.*

THE BURNING OF THE BATTLESHIP *BOMBAY*, 1864

Admiral Henry John Carr, RN. *HMS Bombay*

This vivid account of the loss by fire in 1864 of H.M.S. *Bombay*, with nearly a hundred lives, affords for the first time a complete and authentic story of that great disaster. The survivor who tells the story is Admiral Henry John Carr, who was born in 1839, and joined the Royal Navy in 1852. He attained flag rank in 1894, and retired in 1899 while Admiral-Superintendent of Devonport Dockyard.

Her Majesty's ship *Bombay*, was built so far back as 1827 at Bombay; and was of Indian teak. This wood, though most durable and excellent for naval architecture, is also very inflammable, and her age, nearly forty years, insured every timber in her being extremely dry. The *Bombay* was originally a sailing line of battleship; but in 1860, when our whole Navy had become steamers, she was cut in two, lengthened, and made into a screw ship. About the time she was commissioned for service in South America great pains were being taken, for the prevention of disease, to give ships perfect ventilation in their holds and everywhere. This was carried to a ruinous perfection in the case of the *Bombay*, for there was at all times a thorough draught through open gratings from one partition in the hold to another.

The ships of the Royal Navy have many appliances for the supply of water, and the officers are constantly exercising their crews in the needful duties for extinguishing fire. A disastrous one was of so very rare occurrence on board a man-of-war, even in the old wooden days, that one has to go back some sixty years before the loss of the *Bombay* to find a precedent for the burning of a line of battleship – the *Queen Charlotte*, which took fire and blew up off Leghorn in 1800, with the loss of 673 lives. Therefore, though fire was our most deadly enemy at sea, we always felt perfect confidence in getting the better of it – and that, I need not say, is more than half way towards doing anything in this world. Where men have to save their lives by their own exertions and coolness, a stout heart is everything.

The *Bombay* was the flag-ship of Rear-Admiral Charles Elliott, C.B., on the south-east coast of America; but at the time of the disaster he and his staff were on board H.M.S. *Stromboli*, the *Bombay* having been ordered to sea for a week's exercise with the big guns and in other ways.

We left Monte Video, in the River Plate, early one fine midsummer's morning in December, 1864 – the seasons in south latitudes being reversed – with 655 people on board.

Target practice was the first part of our business that day. After beating the retreat from general quarters at about half-past three in the afternoon, a division on the lower deck were kept at their guns for shell practice. They were my quarters and I was on duty with the division. For the purposes of the exercise the shell-room and the after magazine were kept open. We were just looking out for the target through the lower-deck ports, and I remember so clearly seeing a French merchant-ship going close past us, under all sail.

At this moment, the fire-bell rang, the signal being formed by rapid strokes on the ship's bell. Now, this bell often rang for drill only, and accordingly there were few who suspected that this time the warning was given in grim earnest. But it was soon clear that it was no summons to an ordinary drill, for one of the petty officers who was leaving the hold, where he had been employed all the afternoon in passing shells to the guns, had seen a flame in a far corner, right under the magazine. He had at once run up and rung the bell, and reported what he had seen. Our drills were always done against time, so, with everyone in the ship on the alert, and a great part of the crew still at the guns, it was a matter of only two or three minutes to have six or eight large hoses pouring water wherever directed.

My brother officer on the lower deck at the time was Stirling, the gunnery-lieutenant – he was lost in 1880 with the *Atalanta,* a small sailing frigate which he commanded, and which is supposed to have floundered in the Atlantic with every soul on board.

I superintended the unloading of the guns. The weapons were 8-in. old, muzzle-loading, smooth-bore guns, and the only way to extract a charge was to scoop it out, a task which, with these guns, was very difficult. But we got the charges out, except in the cases of two guns, which were jammed, and in these the powder and shot had to be left – obviously a serious danger in a burning ship.

When I had seen to the guns I went to the pumps aft on the lower deck, and found that there was fire indeed. Smoke was pouring up from below, and was already so dense that it was almost impossible to see. The men who were directing the hoses were constantly relieved, and taken up sick or suffocated. The pumps were heaving bravely round, but the overpowering smoke continued to ascend through the hatchway. The deck became so thick with it that in order to enable us to continue working we had to trice up some of the ports. This could not have been more than five minutes after the outbreak was reported – so fierce and swift was the spread of the flames, due, as I have explained, to the extraordinary dryness of the wood, and the great draught which the prevailing system of ventilation induced, and the imflammable material in the after hold.

Enormous quantities of water were being poured below – literally, tons, for, besides the pumps, there were relays of men with buckets, mess-kettles, and dishes at work, filling and emptying their vessels on to the fire. Hammocks, too, were unleased on deck, and these, with beds and hundreds of blankets, were wetted and sent rapidly below to be used in trying to smother the flames. But the fire, in addition to being so far up in the wing of the hold as to be almost out of reach, had got among a lot of junk – pieces of old cable and cordage – and brooms, and sent out volumes of dense smoke.

One of the pumps was not drawing properly, so I got hold of the carpenter, Mr. Boss, and went down the engine-room hatchway to the orlop deck – the deck below the lower deck and also below the water-line. The orlop deck was thick with smoke in every direction, and so intensely hot that it was impossible to remain there, and we were driven away. Already the orlop deck, which was immediately above the fire, was flooded several inches deep, and so was the after magazine.

Now, had there been a moment for thinking, when it was clear to everyone that a terrible fire was raging and was mastering the ship there would have come the apparent knowledge that the after magazine and the forward magazine contained forty tons of powder each, and that we were in a momentary peril of being blown into the air with the ship; but, happily, we were too busy to think of anything except the work in hand. When I went up to the lower deck again, we found smoke pouring from the "pigeon-holes" – spaces in the old wooden ships which opened from below between the timbers on the lower deck.

One's impressions at such a time are strange and inexplicable. I remember thinking that, even if the worst came to the worst, and the fire really overwhelmed us, we should be quite safe, as the big French ship was so near us; and my own impression was that, bad as things looked, there was more smoke than fire. We went on steadily doing our best between decks, and at the same time a great part of the ship's company was preparing to hoist out the boats – a precaution which was always taken, even for exercise.

The captain (Colin Campbell, whose early death was so sad for all who knew him) and the commander (John Crawford Wilson, who died while Admiral-Superintendent of Devenport Dockyard) now came below to see how matters stood, and it was speedily and abundantly clear that the ship was doomed.

The order "Out boats" had found everything in readiness, and when, on all hands being ordered on deck, I got to my station, which was on the quarter-deck, I found that the boats were being hoisted out. The cutter was out, the barge hooked on and hoisted out on the port side, then the pinnace and first launch on the starboard side, and all the quarter and stern boats were lowered. The first launch was forty-two feet long, the largest in the ship, and had been "raised upon," that is, her gunwales had been heightened so that she could be fitted with a steam-engine. The engine, however – and very fortunately, room being precious – was not in her when she was stowed in-board, because other boats had to go inside her. Besides five boats, which were hanging outside the ship, there were six others, large and small, stowed in-board, and these had to be hoisted out. All were got out square and well except one, the second launch.

The fire had spread so quickly that the smoke now poured up in the waist of the ship and completely cut off one end from the other. An immense help to the flames had been given by the bursting of casks of rum which were stowed in the hold in the compartment next to that in which the fire originated. The bilges, where there was an uninterrupted flow from one end to the other, were flooded with blazing spirits, so that the ship was now on fire literally from bow to stern.

The last large boat was just in the air, though seemingly on fire, when the flames burst on to the quarter-deck, where I then was, and catching an awning over our heads, ran up the rigging, instantly setting every rope and sail in a blaze. The tarred ropes and the awning burnt over our heads with a rush, yards went on end, and spars and burning rigging rattled down. Still we tried to get the second launch over the side, although it looked red-hot with lurid smoke; but its ropes burnt and down it came again; White, the second captain of the maintop, jumping out as it fell.

The very deck on which we stood was now on fire, and a brother lieutenant – now Admiral Sir John Fullerton, who commanded Queen Victoria's yachts, and is an equerry to the King – and myself were the only officers on the quarter-deck, the captain, and the commander having gone to the fore part of the ship. The men on the quarter-deck made a rush for the starboard gangway, where the pinnace was alongside. These men were mostly marines, bandsmen, artificers, craftsmen, and so on – "idlers," as they are called, not being bluejackets. The majority were unable to swim, and it was amongst them that nearly all the deaths occurred.

A large and beautiful white ensign was floating from the peak, union down, in the midst of a thick mass of smoke, as a signal of distress; but the smoke itself was the best announcement of our extremity to three vessels which were in sight, as well as to the land – even to Monte Video in the distance. To swimmers there seemed little danger, even now, for we mostly forgot our greatest danger – the magazines under our feet – and I think that all through it never struck me that I was individually in peril.

Large numbers of men were holding to ropes in the water and to the ship's side. The boats had pulled ahead of the ship with their freights, all but two, the steam launch, a big, unwieldy boat, which was near the stern, and the pinnace, which was close to on the beam, heavily laden with men. The sick had been got into the launch, in which also were a number of officers and men whose duty had been on the poop. Happily none of the sick were seriously ill. The falling of burning ropes and spars reminded Fullerton and myself that it was time to be off; but there was a graver signal than that, which was the bursting of shells between decks. In those days we always had two rounds per gun of live shell stowed in boxes beneath the deck-beams.

The roaring of the flames and the crashing of the bursting shells made it necessary for every man to fend for himself. The result was that there was much mad jumping into the water. Of those who sprang overboard many, being non-swimmers, were paralysed by fear and hurled themselves recklessly into the water. It is a melancholy and significant fact that nearly the whole of the hundred lives which were lost in the catastrophe were those of men who had not learnt to swim, and could not help themselves in the water.

By way of showing the incomprehensible workings of the mind at such a crisis as this, I will mention a strange incident. When Fullerton and myself saw that it was time to go, we got up into the hammock-netting and stripped ourselves before jumping into the sea to swim to one of the boats, the arrangement being that Fullerton should make for the pinnace and I for the launch. We got rid of nearly all our clothes, and then the two of us took our watches and chains and other little things we valued and secured them in the netting, believing, even then, that we should be able to return to the ship and get them! On the anniversary of the disaster Sir John and I regularly exchange letters, and in his last communication he said how well he remembers this curious mutual act at such a time.

Fullerton safely swam after the pinnace and I got into the mainchains and saw Blake, the doctor, jump aboard out of one of the ports under the poop and make for the launch. I encouraged the men who were hanging on below me by telling them that they were quite safe and that the launch would come and pick them up. Two

Just then a shell burst behind us on the main deck, and we all jumped involuntarily into the water.

midshipmen, named Strange and Hamilton, were with me. Strange, poor fellow, was afterwards navigating lieutenant with Stirling when he was lost with the *Atalanta*. I told Strange to stand by to swim for the launch; and as for Hamilton – who could not swim – I assured him that he was safe enough, and that we would get him into the launch, which in due time we did.

Just then a shell burst behind us on the main deck, and we all jumped involuntarily into the water. I made for the launch, and saw Mr. Boss, the carpenter, – an enormously fat and very famous old gentleman – who helped me to haul over the lofty bows. Another celebrated person who was in the launch was Giddy, the chief boatswain's mate. He had in his pocket his watch-bill, a little list of the men of the ship's company, which turned out to be the only list by which we could muster the men afterwards. Every other record of the people on board was lost.

With great difficulty we managed to get the launch up to the ship, having only a few oars, and the current being very strong. The *Bombay's* anchors had been burnt from their fastenings, and so she had anchored herself. We got in, however, and rescued all the men who were still hanging to the ship's side. I was too busy with this work to look much about me, but was constantly reminded by others less so in the stern of the boat, that the mainmast was falling, the magazine about to blow up, guns going off, and shells exploding. Watts, the master, and myself were therefore glad enough to shove off the moment we had lugged the last terrified non-swimmer over the bows.

On clearing the ship I, for the first time, took in the perfect ruin from which we had escaped. The hull was burning from end to end, flames were roaring out of most of the ports, there was the constant explosions of shell, the mizzen-mast seemed about to fall one way and the foremast another, all the stays being burnt, and the masts themselves were on fire in many places. The main-mast, a towering mass of spars, two hundred feet high, and weighing altogether some eighty tons, was leaning right over the spot where we had been, and in another minute fell across the side, and would infallibly have smashed our boat and us too! Surely here a Kind Hand had held it back till we had finished our work.

We had plenty to do, for, as we were the only boat astern of the ship, all the men who were floating on bits of spars, gratings, hammocks, etc., came our way with the tide, and were picked up. We found Poë, a little midshipman, swimming bravely about. He is now a rear-admiral, commanding in the East Indies. Then there was Ramsden, another midshipman, on a breaker; and Kelly, the first-lieutenant, and engineer McGarahan were adrift on a hatch, which had been thrown overboard. Kelly was very sick, having been stifled in the hold of the ship, and simply lay under the thwarts all the evening. He lived to be an admiral and Superintendent at Chatham. Forrest, another lieutenant, and King, the master-at-arms, were on a spar, very exhausted – Forrest so much so that he murmured: "Don't touch me – I'm too far gone!" I think he is dead, poor chap. We picked up a man, a leading stoker, who had got under a spar, and was being rolled round and round with it. The spar was on his chest, and the ducking would soon have drowned him if we had not pulled him into the boat.

Our clumsy boat was by this time drifting further and further astern, and as we could not see any further survivor floating about we dropped our anchor, and Watts, the dear old master – a rank now replaced by that of navigating lieutenant – suggested that we should offer a prayer for our deliverance. He himself recited aloud the Lord's Prayer and the Prayer for Those at Sea – which were probably all that anybody could recall at such a time. Watts still enjoys an honoured old age, after being master of the Queen's yacht and Staff-Captain of Portsmouth Dockyard.

We had a very mixed crew in our boat of about one hundred. Many people had got into her off the *Bombay's* stern. Amongst them was a middy – Stevenson – a lightweight, luckily, who, in his hurry, jumped off the taffrail, first pitching his sextant down. The height could not have been less than thirty feet, and he alightened on the heads of those who were in the boat. Wonderful to relate, he did no damage – perhaps because the heads were so closely together.

I only saw one jump taken, but it was a very sad attempt. One poor fellow who was in the boat which we did not manage to hoist out, leapt out of her when the smoke became unbearably thick, but instead of alighting on the deck he went plump down a hatchway covered with a tarpaulin, into the heart of the fire, and must have been destroyed instantly. He was one of the few who perished inside the ship – we only knew certainly of two others, men who said they would go and try to save some of their valuables. They went below and were never seen again. Nothing could live in such a furnace.

Falling anchors, spars, etc., killed several men under the boats, but the bulk of the ninty-two who were lost were drowned because of their inability to swim. Having anchored our boat when we found that there was no more lives to swim, we got her to rights. Those who had been lucky enough to escape with their clothes on lent some of their garments to the less fortunate survivors, of whom a number were naked.

The three masts had by this time fallen and the hull was rapidly burning down. Still, to our wonder, neither of the magazines blew up. The smaller boats had all clustered ahead of the ship, and after distributing their cargoes volunteers were called for, so that a boat could make the very perilous attempt to save those who were still clinging under the bows. These volunteers instantly came forward and made two most hazardous trips and safely took off all who had not been carried down by falling wreckage. These rescued men were unable to swim, and Stirling, who was amongst them, saw many a poor fellow sink. Among other risks of this undertaking was that of encountering a stream of molten lead which the intense heat was causing to run from the bows, and the marks of which were left on more than one survivor. On this dangerous service, which was carried out in the most gallant fashion, Mandeville, then a sub-lieutenant, greatly distinguished himself. He was especially promoted for this service, and the commander was also specially promoted for his conduct.

So incredibly fast had the flames taken possession of the whole ship that certainly within an hour of the outbreak the mainmast had fallen, and it can hardly have been more than half that time before we were driven out of her, having hoisted all our boats out.

It was now about six o'clock, and getting dark and cold, too, so that I was very glad to have a shirt from one of the dry men and to put my legs through the sleeves for trousers, my own soaked flannel and shirt having been till then my only garments.

The pinnace had been relieved of part of her immense cargo of one hundred and fifty men by a pilot boat – she was so seriously overladen that she was only kept afloat by the men making an extra gunwale with their backs, and so keeping the water, or rather the lop, out. It was lucky, indeed, therefore, that the pilot boat, which had been hovering about, came and took some of the people out of her. We communicated with the pinnace and divided our store of small masts and sails which we had picked up, thrown from the boats ahead, and then made sail. Monte Video, which we could see in the distance, fifteen miles off. We used blankets, bedcovers, awnings, and anything else we could lay hands on as sails.

All Monte Video was astir by this time, and ship after ship of various nations came tearing out. There were three sailing ships in sight, an English brig called the *Water Lily*, which came down to windward and hove to among the small boats ahead; a Hanoverian brig, which was standing out from inshore, and the French ship, but she was a long way to leeward, although beating up towards us. The ships were too late to help in saving life; but they put us sooner into safety, for our heavily-laden boats would ill have stood the sort of sea that gets up so quickly in those shallow waters, and which, as a matter of fact, swiftly followed our landing.

The pinnace and our own boat were picked up by a passenger steamer, the *Rio de la Plata*, which was just starting for Beunos Aires. She was really a mail boat, and we were very glad to get on board, especially as a Brazilian steamer had calmly steamed past, without taking any notice of our distress or offering help. We went below into the saloon and had some grog; but we were soon driven out by the entrance of a host of ladies who had come to dinner. Our rig was not suitable for mixed company!

We went on deck, and were just up in time to see the end of the *Bombay*. There was, at each end of her, as I have explained, a magazine containing some forty tons of powder. We could not have believed it possible that their walls of wood and mortar could have so long resisted the furnace they were in. Just five hours had passed since the discovery of the fire under the after magazine, and it is marvellous that the ship escaped so long.

Suddenly we saw a fan-shaped flame shoot up from the dull red spot where the *Bombay* was burning, then ten miles from us. In two minutes there was total darkness, and everything that was left of our home and its contents, as well as all we owned, was buried under the muddy waters of the River Plate. This was about 8.30 p.m.

When we got into Monte Video, as all our own ships had gone out, we proceeded to the French storeship *Fortune*, and our friends the French, with whom we were on the most excellent terms on that station, overwhelmed us with kindnesses, from the admiral downwards.

The admiral – he was an enormously stout old gentleman – gave me one of his shirts, which I kept for many years, the captain of the *Rio de la Plata* presented me with a pair of trousers – he must, like many others, have given away all his kit – and so we were clothed and fed and looked after in the most generous fashion. A large part of us, indeed, were put up for a week by our French friends on board their ships, and some also by the Italian frigate *Regina*.

We mustered the crews of the launch and the pinnace and found that in these two boats alone we had no fewer than 180 men. We could have taken a great many more in the launch, but the pinnace was chock full. The *Stromboli,* our largest remaining vessel, with the admiral and his staff on board, came in about eleven o'clock. A midnight we went on board her, and roughly estimated that ninety of our own number were missing. This proved to be nearly correct, the actual number being ninty-two, including a couple of officers – Smallhorn, the surgeon and Franklin, the boatswain – who were lost under the *Bombay's* bows, and some fifteen seamen. The rest were marines, etc.

Dr. Smallhorn's death was as tragic as it was remarkable. He was a non-swimmer, and, like most of those who were similarly helpless, he was watching and waiting for a chance to escape by being taken off in one of the boats. He was sitting on the sheet-anchor, outside the ship, when it was burnt from its securing-chains, and he went to the bottom with the great mass of iron which formed the anchor.

The *Bombay* was burnt on a nasty, squally night, making us glad to be clear of the boats, but on the following night it was blowing a regular *pampero* - one of the fierce local gales in which our crowded boat would have had no chance of living.

Early in the morning after the disaster Stirling and Skinner, a midshipman, were sent home by the French mail boat to report the disaster, the news of which was telegraphed to England from Lisbon – in those days the nearest cable station. I was ordered to take a party of fifty men to the Lamport and Holt steamer *Herschel,* which had been chartered to bring us home, to clear her lower deck of hides and bones, and otherwise prepare her for our reception. We left Monte Video in a week's time for England, and on our way out passed the scene of the disaster. The *Bombay's* bowsprit, held by its wire rigging, was bobbing awash, the ship having sunk in only seven fathoms – forty-two feet – of water. Even that soon disappeared, and what had been a noble battleship was covered by the mud.

We picked up one body, that of a marine, and buried it. That was the only one that was ever heard of, for, strangely enough, no corpses went ashore.

On the passage home every effort was made to find some reason for the fire, and the court-martial by which we were all tried got no further towards a solution of the mystery. To this day not one of the survivors can offer a satisfactory suggestion on the point.

Admiral Henry J Carr, RN.

Gunner Israel Harding, VC.

THE BOMBARDMENT OF ALEXANDRIA, 1882

Gunner Israel Harding VC, RN. *HMS Alexandra*

In his dispatch of July 14th, 1882, Admiral Sir F. Beauchamp Seymour, Commander-in-Chief on the Mediterranean Station, briefly described the most thrilling incident of the bombardment of Alexandria and one of the finest acts for which the Victoria Cross was ever awarded. "Captain Hotham, of the *Alexandria*," he wrote, "has specially brought to my notice a deed of valour performed by Mr. Israel Harding, the gunner of the ship, who probably saved many lives by lifting and placing in a tub of water a ten-inch shell with a burning fuse which had passed through the ship's side and lodged on the main deck." For that act Mr. Harding was at once promoted chief gunner, and was afterwards awarded the Victoria Cross. The bombardment began early on the morning of July 11th, 1882, and within eleven hours the city was in ruins through the terrible fire of the British naval guns, at ranges varying from 1000 to 4000 yards. The British loss was remarkably slight, but the Egyptians had nearly 2000 killed and wounded.

The man is what the boy was, which is another way of saying that the boy is the father of the man. I was born to the sea and bred to danger, so that when in after years I did that thing of which people have spoken so much – and far more than it deserves to be talked about – I acted without a thought of any recognition whatsoever, or that I was doing anything beyond my duty.

I am something of a veteran now, past my three-score-and-ten years, and more than two decades have gone since I heard the cashing of the guns at Alexandria; but I can say as truly now as I have asserted constantly, that I do not consider that I did anything whatever extraordinary. The world has been pleased to think differently, and I have become resigned to the world's way of looking at the matter – but not accustomed even yet to the wonderful stories which people I have told concerning me, and the still more startling pictures which artists have drawn of me and my achievement.

I have been made to do the most grotesque and impossible things, not the least marvellous being that of getting a 10-inch shell into a pail which could not hold it – a trick of which a conjuror might be proud; and so I am going to tell you what I actually did on that famous day when big gun flashed against big gun at Alexandria, when armoured battleships tried conclusions with powerful land forts and repeated the triumphs of Algiers and Navarino.

The bombardment came to me as a matter of course, for I have the blood of sailors and fighting ancestors in me – and I was born on Trafalgar Day in 1833. That means something surely to a British sailor. My father was Queen's pilot at Portsmouth for many years, and my paternal grandfather was a Portsmouth King's pilot, while my mother's father was a mastermariner. It all counts, don't you think? At any rate it counted with me. Then, as for my upbringing – as a small boy I enlarged my knowledge of the alphabet by using a bit of stick on the sands not far from the spot where Nelson embarked for his last great fight at sea. I continued my education at the Bethel and at a private school, where I was taught navigation, until I was fourteen. I was then apprenticed to a pilot. My father at that time was master of H.M. steam vessel *Echo,* and I began my career of forty years in the Royal Navy as a cabin boy in that quaint ship.

Almost at once I was plunged into an exciting experience, which was of immense service to me in after-life, because it was discipline that hardened me to danger. H.M.S. *Sphinx* was stranded at the back of the Isle of Wight, and we with other ships went to help her. One of the assisting cutters was capsized, and several men were drowned. I had many narrow escapes myself, as I went to and from the wreck whenever I had the chance during the four months it took us to get the ship afloat and into Portsmouth.

In May, 1849, I joined H.M.S. *Arrogant,* and served in her until 1853, and then joined H.M.S. *Excellent,* the Naval Gunnery School at Portsmouth. It fell to my duty to go with others to test a gun which was mounted in H.M.S. *Skylark,* the target being an old wooden frigate. It was a rifled weapon, quite a new invention, and nobody could tell what sort of tricks it would play, so, after the gun was laid, everyone was sent either below or into a boat alongside, for fear of accidents. That was before the age of electrical appliances, and the gun was fired with a long lanyard reaching to the boat on the off side of the ship. Everything had gone so well that it was meant, after the next round, to keep us all in our proper stations. The hand-spikemen, however – myself and three others – remained at the gun to keep the training on till the very last moment before firing. We had just time to pop down the fore-hatch when the gun was fired.

Then a most astounding thing happened – the weapon burst! The muzzle and chase went over the side, and one half of the cascabel flew over the bow, cutting the foremast in two, and bringing it crashing down above our heads; the other half passed through the funnel, crashing through the mainmast, and bringing that down, too; then it passed over the stern.

It was a remarkable and unexpected accident, and, but for the fact that we were all below, the loss of life would have been very heavy. As it was, not a man was hurt – but how different a story if the disaster had occurred with the next round, when faith in the rifled freak would have been fully established!

I made my first acquaintance with war at the bombardment of Sweaborg in 1855, when I was serving my second year in the Baltic, and that was another very useful bit of training for the bombardment of Alexandria. While serving in H.M.S. *Alexandra* in 1882, we were carrying out the usual work of the British Fleet in those days and those waters – policing the Mediterranean. Affairs were pretty critical in Egypt, and we were constantly on the watch for trouble.

On Sunday, April 30th, we were quietly anchored at Corfu, expecting the usual inspection and service, but instead the ships unmoored and steamed out to sea, making for Suda Bay in Candia. This sudden movement showed that something was in the wind, especially as the admiral had shifted his flag from the *Alexandra* to the *Invincible,* and sailed for Alexandria. We learnt that Arabi Pasha was the cause of the mischief, and he put himself into a position of enormous strength - so strong that he felt he could defy even the British ships of war. He was a masterful man, and made himself a master, too, and a dictator. Earthworks and batteries were being constructed, and our admiral demanded that they should be removed, threatening to bombard Alexandria if he were disobeyed.

The work continued, and our chief kept his word.

He was very precise in his plans, and promised to open fire on the Tuesday, July 11th. Our greatest fear was then that something would happen to prevent him from keeping his vow, a fear so great that when it was rumoured that a number of Egyptian officers, who had come in a steam launch from the shore, were suing for peace, many prayers were uttered for them – but directed to the wrong quarter. We thought they wanted peace, and condemned them for interfering busybodies and spoil-sports.

For many reasons that quiet July night off the coast of the land of the Pharaohs was a memorable one. There was a subdued excitement which affected and possessed everybody. Would there really be fighting? Would the Egyptians cave in at the last moment and disappoint all of us who wanted a fight? These and a hundred other questions were asked and eagerly discussed, but in the very middle of the night they vanished from consideration, for the pipe went, "Up anchor," and we knew what that meant – bombardment. Then the bugles sounded for action, and every officer and man went to his station, full of confidence and courage. Each captain had been supplied by the admiral with a copy of the order of battle, and I daresay that in the solemn darkness these were scanned by many an anxious eye.

Even as we steamed slowly and majestically on, cleared for action, there was the fear that at the last moment the enemy would abandon their forts and guns and let us have a bloodless victory; but as daylight broke we plainly saw that they were determined to try the test of battle. It was now that the order was given to load our guns with common shell.

So that you might have a clear idea of the fight, let me sketch a very short general outline of it. The Commander-in-Chief made two attacks: one by the *Sultan*, *Superb* and *Alexandra* on the northern face of Ras-el-Teen, supported by the fire from the after-turret of the *Inflexible*, anchored off the entrance of the Corvette Pass, thus enfilading the lighthouse batteries; the other by the *Invincible*, *Monarch* and *Penelope* from inside the reefs, helped by the fire of the *Inflexible's* foremost turret and the *Téméraire*, which was near the Boghaz, or chief pass leading to Alexandria Harbour. The *Helicon* and *Condor* were repeating ships, and the *Beacon*, *Bittern*, *Cygnet*, and *Decoy* were employed during the day according to orders.

My own ship, the *Alexandra*, led the van, the *Superb* and *Sultan* following. We steamed slowly along in front of the forts, and as we did the officers of divisions pointed out each fort to the captains of the guns, especially cautioning them to aim only at these points. Nothing, you see, was to be left to chance. There had been plenty of time to prepare a programme, and now there was to be no excuse for not carrying out that programme efficiently.

We had got our anchors up at four o'clock; now it was seven, and three hours of tense expectation were followed by the thrilling and gladly-welcomed signal from the

Invincible to us, the van ship, to begin the battle. Almost instantly one of our main battery guns crashed and sent its shell across the still waters towards Fort Curostos.

It was a wonderful sensation to feel that we had actually, from our own ship, opened the battle, and then to watch and wait for the enemy's reply. Even yet the flag might flutter down in token of surrender; but there was no reply of any sort for several minutes. This uncertainty would never do; our Commander-in-Chief must know exactly what the purpose of the Egyptians was, and so a second shot was fired, a solemn crash and boom and challenge from our armoured sides, and a big shot's dull roar across the placid waters.

There was no need to wonder what the enemy's intention was – he meant to fight, and to fight to the death. From turrets, tarbettes, main and central batteries, and conning-towers, watching eyes saw lines of vivid flashes and belching of smoke from battery and earthwork, and listening ears soon heard the accompanying thunder of the ordnance. It was a swift and almost magic change from perfect peace to the very hell of war; for as soon as the shore roared back defiance every gun in the fleet that could be brought to bear was discharged, and the forts burst into simultaneous fire and thunder.

Each ship fired independently, each captain of a gun aimed for a certain mark, each gun's crew set hard to work in this contest of pounding to see who could pound the hardest, and each ship's company strove to score a first place in markmanship. Round and about us elongated and spherical projectiles hissed and screamed, some falling considerably short of the ships and others whistling and crashing through their rigging and cutting away portions of the running gear.

To me, brought up in the old school, which was practically a continuation of Nelson's navy, accustomed as I had been during the Russian War to fight with the same sort of muzzle-loading weapon that won for us Trafalgar, it was marvellous and fascinating to observe the quickness of our heavy breech-loading fire, and to know that our cannon-loading was the heaviest in naval history.

If this was the feeling of myself and others who were in the thick of the fighting, able to see only part of the bombardment, what must it have been to the crews of the merchantmen which were anchored out of range and witnessed the whole of the struggle? They expressed their feelings in rounds and rounds of excited cheering, just as spectators might applaud a thrilling play.

The shot and shell which crashed against our armour broke up; but those which struck the weaker portions of the ship penetrated and did a lot of mischief. Our own practice, as we could see from time to time when the smoke cleared, was deadly and demoralising. Every shot seemed to strike home, and forts were shattered and gunners destroyed in a way that showed the utter hopelessness of resistance. But the Egyptians had warmed to their work, and their fire was becoming very accurate.

We in the *Alexandra* were in the very thick of things, and had just as much excitement as I, for one, could carry, and as Gunner I was here, there, and everywhere, particularly about the magazines, and that is exciting duty enough when you know that at any moment a shell may come and explode your powder and sky you in fragments.

We, in the *Alexandra*, were in the very thick of things.

It is the commonest of commonplaces to say of British troops and sailors that they went into action as steadily as if they had been drilling or parading; but at the bombardment of Alexandria this was literally the case. You could not have supposed from the demeanour of officers and men that they were about to enter upon a struggle which would assuredly mean to some of them the loss of the number of their mess.

Before the battle itself we had concerts in the fleets, and nervous people cannot play and sing as we did both. Then we had little lectures, too – short, brisk discourses on the topics of the moment. Of these the one I best remember was delivered by our excellent Commander Thomas, whose subject was: "What is a Crisis?" If Arabi had heard the lecture, and still more, if he had listened to the comments on it, he would, I doubt not, have remarked gloomily: "This is one for me, anyway," because discourse and criticism had some remarkably free allusions to the prime power of the mischief.

That spirit of cheerfulness and indifference was maintained throughout the action. Bear in mind that, fighting as we were fighting, only one side of the ship could fire at a time. This meant that, as we steamed along the torts, half the men, those on the side of the ship which was not engaged, had no fighting to do. And how do you suppose they employed their time? In playing cards!

Yes, it is actually true that while the guns on the other side of the ship belched death and crashed and thundered, these men unconcernedly amused themselves. They did that until the ship turned round and so brought their own guns into action. Then they sprang to their stations and blazed away, but not before they had handed over their cards to the powder-grimed men, whose hot and smoking weapons were taking a short rest.

I do not think that if I spoke pages I could give you a better idea than this circumstance affords of the perfect coolness and assurance of our men at Alexandria. To play cards while the ship is shivering with the crash of her artillery, when there is such a roar and racket that the very hearing is deadened, when any instant a shell might come and destroy a gun's crew, or even the ship itself – to do that, I say, shows perfect courage and discipline. At Alexandria it was proof that the old Nelson spirit was still the moving power in the British Navy.

Ah! I knew the question was inevitable! How did I win my own Victoria Cross, and what were the actual circumstances that led to the award? Well, I do not like to talk about my own doings, but since you will have it I will do the best I can.

The *Alexandra* was naturally a special target, and there was plenty of her to hit. The exitement began early. A shell came through the port side forward, and, bursting close to the sheep-pen, killed the only occupant; another cut away a stout iron stanchion, and, narrowly missing the captain – he is now Admiral of the Fleet Sir C.F. Hotham – and the staff-commander, carried off a piece of the fore funnel casing. Another shell struck the steam launch, and exploding in her smashed her to atoms, killing one man and wounding two others. Again the captain had a very narrow escape – there were many close shaves that day.

It was just at this time, when I had been through the upper and main batteries to make sure of everything necessary being supplied, and I was told that the empty hoppers of the Nordenfelt guns, which were being worked by the signalman on the poop, had not been returned to the magazine for refilling. I went to the poop, and Commander Thomas, who was standing on the quarter-deck netting, asked me what I wanted. I told him, and had just left him to go down the ladder to the after-deck, when a shell crashed through the port bulwarks under his feet, and striking a metal stanchion burst in his cabin, destroying everything.

I ought perhaps to explain that the gunnery lieutenant, the Hon. M. Bourke, who was afterwards the captain of the *Victoria* when she was rammed by the *Camperdown*, was very ill, and confined to the cockpit throughout the engagement, so the gunnery duties devolved on me.

I was recovering from the shock of that explosion and was starting to descend the hatchway on the next deck leading to the after-magazine, when a shell penetrated the ship's side, passing through the torpedo lieutenant's cabin. Then it struck against the iron coamings of the engine-room, rebounded round the rifle-racks, and lodged close to a large tub of water which had been placed in readiness to put out any fire that might occur.

Some men who formed the fire party saw the fuse burning and shouted: "A shell! A shell!" which is about the most jumpy alarm you can raise in battle. It is a signal to make you skip, and I turned round swiftly and saw the awful missile at my feet. At such a time a man does not stop to think, and I stooped and picked up the shell and instinctively placed it in the tub of water, although the chances are even that a fuse will not be extinguished by such means as that. Yet what I wished for happened – the water did its work, the fuse ceased to burn, and the projectile became a harmless object.

One might have smiled to look at it – yet how vast were its possiblities! It was a ten-inch spherical projectile, and contained a bursting charge of twelve pounds of gunpowder. The fuse, which I still possess, is four and a half inches long, and seems to have had an inch or more sawn off at the bottom so that it would burst on reaching the target aimed at. About half the composition of the fuse was burnt away, and in another second or two, if it had not been for the tub of water – but why picture what did not happen?

You do not think that is enough for the incident, and that I should dwell upon it at greater length? Well, let me give you a better idea of what it all meant. Twelve pounds of gunpowder will do an enormous amount of damage if properly directed, and this particular shell was just as nicely placed for mischief as any shell could have been.

For one thing it was in a confined space, being on the main deck, which was equal to being in a large room. There were plenty of officers and men about as prey for its performance, and so that nothing should be lacking to complete its possibilities of havoc, there was within reach of its flames the after-magazine with its twenty-five tons of gunpowder – and not the strongest ship that mortal man has built will survive the explosion of a quantity like that.

I had the awful thing in my hands. What was I to do with it, how get rid of it? I could not thrust or throw it back through the jagged hole by which it had entered the side, nor could I hurl it overboard, because we were in a confined space between decks. There was only this slender, forlorn hope of the tub, and into the tub the missile went. It was a heavy burden, but you do not notice weight at such a crisis as that.

To add to the peril of the situation, eighty-five pound charges of powder were being passed up from the magazine for the upper and main battery guns. These charges were being carried past the very spot where the shell was burning, so that if it had exploded it would have had the additional help of a very fine bursting charge.

So, you see, every possible circumstance contributed to the chances of destruction, and yet they were circumvented on the spur of the moment because of the more or less chance presence of a tub of water, and because of that early training in a hard school of which I have spoken.

One striking and amusing thing comes back to my mind. Over the tub was a tank containing drinking water for the ward-room, and on the tank was painted the warning "Waste not." Perhaps the way in which the moral precept had sunk into my mind may have had something to do with the promptness with which I plunged my live shell into the receptive tub. Never, at any rate, I think, was better use made of water than I made of that.

Our escape was by a hair's breadth, but we were far too busy to think about it then. The fight was raging furiously and guns ashore were being dismounted and magazines blown up. We had a very good opportunity of seeing what an explosion of powder meant, for a shell from the *Superb* blew up the main magazine at Fort Ada. There was a terrific report, and enormous mischief was done. This particular fort had been troubling us greatly, and we instantly felt the relief of its disappearance – so much, indeed, that we were able to pipe our water to dinner, which had to be taken in the batteries, as our men's mess-deck was in a ruinous state, the tables and stools having been destroyed by shells.

Fort Ada was a special target that day, and it gave evidence of the appalling devastation which modern big guns can cause. The seaward face of Port Pharos was the target for the eight-ton guns of the *Inflexible,* and from time to time, above all other noises of the battle, we heard the boom of these artillery monsters. Each shell that was sent weighed 1700 pounds – that is to say, more than three-quarters of a ton – and the flight of the projectile made a sound which has been very fairly compared with the rumble of a railway train.

In connection with one of these weapons, an act of the greatest courage and resource was performed on board the *Inflexible* by an engine-room artificer. The vent of one of her 80-ton guns became choked so badly that the weapon was completely useless, and so that it could be brought again into action the man had to get into it. This would not have been an easy or pleasant performance at any time, but it was doubly disagreeable and dangerous now, when there was great risk of suffocation from the accumulated gases. Besides, it meant that he had to be forced in, very much as if he had been a shot or shell.

With the help of the rammer he was driven up the bore of the gun, the diameter of which was sixteen inches, as far as the powder-chamber, and there and then he cleared the vent. Then he was hauled back by means of a rope which had been fastened round his ankles, and had his reward in finding that the gun could be brought into action once more.

A good deal is always said of the changed condition of modern fights at sea. Well, ships and guns have altered, but the officers and men do not change, and Alexandria gave proof of the reckless daring which signalised the old days of sailors and wooden walls. There was, for instance, the famous achievement of Lord Charles Beresford, who, seeing the mischief which was being done by two ten-inch rifled guns from the forts, steamed audaciously up within range of them and drew off their fire from the other ships, although a single lucky shot would have utterly destroyed him and his gunboat, the *Condor*.

Then there was the no less valiant action of a dozen officers and men from the *Invincible,* one of whom was our Flag-Lieutenant, the Hon.H. Lambton, who landed through a dangerous surf and spiked some guns, destroying others with dynamite, and all under a heavy fire. It was a young seaman of the *Invincible,* too, who, when his wounded leg had been amputated, hopped about with it and displayed it proudly to his comrades. That was certainly the sort of thing they did in Nelson's days.

For more than ten hours we pounded with our guns, and then the enemy had had enough. Their forts were in ruins, their guns were smashed or useless, their dead and wounded were everywhere, and the city was already swarming with deserters and looters, ruffians who spared neither man, woman, nor child, and who set fire to every building they came across. It was a lurid and terrible crowning of our own bombardment, and overwhelmed me with awe as I watched the flames shoot skyward in the darkness.

On our way to our anchorage we were met by an American frigate, whose crew had manned her rigging and cheered us enthusiastically while their band played the British National Anthem.

DISASTER ON *HMS CALLIOPE*, 1889, AND ON *HMS VICTORIA*, 1893

Botswain William Marshfield, RN.

The teller of this thrilling double story, Mr. William Marshfield, R.N., has the extraordinary record of having shared in two events which are unparalleled in the annals of the British Navy, the saving of H.M.S. *Calliope* during a terrible hurricane at Samoa in 1889, and the loss of H.M.S. *Victoria*, which was rammed and sunk by H.M.S. *Camperdown* in the Mediterranean in 1893. As if that were not enough, Mr. Marshfield was actually ordered to join H.M.S. *Captain*, which foundered inthe Bay of Biscay in 1870 with six hundred officers and men. He entered the Royal Navy from the mercantile marine, and retired after more than forty years' adventurous service. Mr. Marshfield was boatswain not only of the *Calliope*, but also of the *Victoria*.

I am a superstitious man, a man with what are called presentiments. Everybody knows what presentiments are, but no one has ever been able to explain them. You are overwhelmed with a sense of coming evil – that is what presentiment means.

In the early part of 1870 I was drafted to *HMS Captain*. From the moment that order was given I was so filled with a foreboding of disaster that I went the length of vowing that rather than go to sea in the ship I would leave the Service. It was no good reasoning with or laughing at me; it was useless to tell me that the *Captain* was designed by a famous man, and that he himself had so much faith in his vessel that he was going to sea in her. I refused to be laughed or talking out of my forgivings, and at last, by a stroke of luck, I got transferred to H.M.S. *Excellent*, gunnery ship.

The *Captain* sailed a few months afterwards, and during the night capsized in the Bay of Biscay, carrying with her nearly all her officers and men, as well as her confiding designer. Only the watch on deck, less than a score of souls, was saved.

Twenty-three years later I was ordered to join H.M.S. *Victoria*, the finest and most costly ship of war the world had ever seen. Again I had my deep misgiving. Why, I cannot tell; but before going on board I turned to some of the dock policemen and told them of my fear that something serious would happen. They laughed at me – and with good reason, because, so far as human skill and a nation's wealth could make her so, the battleship was perfect.

But I am getting on too fast. I have to go back to another story, which has nothing to do with presentiments, which was not a personal disaster at all, as disasters go, and which was yet an experience so harassing, so overwhelming, that I have never hesitated to say, and do not hesitate to repeat, that I would rather go through any other crisis of my life than live those awful hours again.

And that dismaying trial was the saving of H.M.S. *Calliope* in the hurricane at Samoa. I say *the* hurrican, because there is only one that occurred in those parts which sailors speak and remember.

Apia Harbour is in Samoa, and Samoa is in the South Seas. In March, 1889, the tiny harbour was crowded with warships, brought together by a political crisis of which I need not say anything. There was the *Calliope,* a British third-class cruiser of 2770 tons – she is still in the Navy; the *Trenton, Vandalia,* and *Nipsic,* American; and the *Alder, Olga,* and *Eber,* German.

There we were, bottled up in a perfect trap of coral reefs, bunched together with the red fangs on three sides of us and the vast open sea in front. The reefs are terrible things at all times, and doubly awful when you are forced to lie so near them that you could hit them with a stone. At low water they were dry, with a surf always breaking on them from the tremendous rollers of the Pacific.

The hurrican did not sweep down upon us without warning. The barometer told us that something stiff was coming, and, as a matter of fact, we had three hard gales as appetisers. But with lower yards and topmasts struck, and the engines steaming so as to relieve the strain on the anchors, we had ridden the breezes out snugly enough. People ashore told us that the fall meant rain, and not wind, and we believed them. We were glad to do it. But the glass went down and down, and the sky grew perfectly black.

There was a dead, depressing calm; but on March 15 the wind rose and freshened, blowing almost straight into the harbour. It gained strength as the night came on, and all the time it was slowly working round so that it blew directly upon us. By midnight we were being lashed by the wind and smothered by the waves; but we were getting used to that sort of thing, and held up to it with our anchors down and the engines going ahead. So fierce was the wind that you would have thought it could not increase; yet it was tame compared with the hurricane which developed and raged throughout the middle and the morning watches.

Enormous seas drove in, meeting the waves which had been hurled against the shore behind us and cast back towards the harbour mouth. The harbour literally boiled. There was an appalling commotion – the screaming of the wind, the roaring of the waves, the thunder of the breakers on the beach and reefs, and the groaning and straining of the cruiser mingling in a deafening noise. And with it all there was the intense darkness and the pitiless rain. Men were furiously shouting to each other; but what could human voices do in such a storm as that? Why, your very words were driven back through your teeth.

No human vision in such a pall of blackness, such a smother of sea and rain, could tell whether our ship was riding safely or was being driven to destruction on the reefs, nor could the acute hearing tell one howling, booming sound from another. Yet we hoped for the best, until the heaving of the lead and the slacking of our stern hawser told us the fearful truth that we were not holding our own, in spite of our strong anchors and powerful engines, and that the *Calliope* was being forced back.

There was no need to tell anyone what would happen in such a case. There was not a soul who did not understand the smashing power of those gigantic breakers – hills of water with the whole strength of the Pacific behind them, not a man who did not realise exactly what it meant to be hurled on to the huge coral teeth which mouthed and frothed at us on all sides except one. And on that side were swamping seas!

What happened during that unspeakable night was mercifully hidden from us until the daylight came – if you can describe as daylight an atmosphere which with mingled wind and sea and spume was like a yellow fog. Then the spectacle was so awful that we who were still safe might well have wished for darkness again to hide it from our view.

Disasters had begun early – calamities which were all the more piteous because no help or courage could avert them. Two foreign merchant ships had collided – smashed upon each other in the welter. One had sunk instantly, and the other went down soon afterwards. Then the *Eber*, which was a gunboat, was picked up, hurled on to the reefs, smashed to pieces, and every soul on board drowned except five, who were saved by a miracle. They found themselves ashore – and that was all they or anybody else could tell.

That was the beginning of things, the opening of that fierce, protracted battle with the storm in which all knew we were engaged, for the warships were bundled in a heap, straining madly at their anchors and already breaking away, driving towards the reefs and destruction. Besides the ships of war there were the merchant vessels, so that there was quite a fleet of various sorts of craft dragging together in hopeless confusion. And all these ships were targets for the storm, which charged upon and battered them with a fury that was diabolical.

The night wore on and the morning was fully with us. The hurricane had driven us slowly but resistlessly to within a few feet of the reef astern, and the huge seas were burying our ship as they roared in. The other ships were tumbling towards us and on top of us, and it was clear that our only hope of salvation lay either in gaining the open sea or beaching the *Caliope* on one particular sandy patch. The former hope, forlorn as it seemed, was the best, and Captain Kane took hold of it. You can only appreciate the courage of that resolve when you understand that the chances were that our ship would not answer her helm, would not steer, and would therefore be hurled back and smashed.

The Staff Engineer was roused up for every ounce of steam he could give, and our only remaining cable was slipped, the whole force of the six boilers was transferred to the cylinders, and in turn to the propeller. At her best the *Calliope* had done nearly fifteen knots – that is, about seventeen miles – an hour, with nearly four thousand horse-power; but now, fighting for her very life, with the engines straining and the machinery in parts almost red-hot, she literally did not appear to move. She kept head to sea and was deluged by masses of green water, and she kept just clear of the reefs astern. We remained afloat and headed to sea, and for the first time that was all we could claim to be doing. Repeatedly we shipped solid water so heavily that many a vessel would have foundered under the mere crushing of it.

With the engines exerting every ounce of their power the *Calliope* at length managed to do about a mile an hour, but for a long time after we began our forlorn fight she seemed not to move an inch. Imagine our triumphant exultation when we felt that she was really gaining speed enough to give her steerage-way, and that there was the faintest chance, but a chance still, of struggling out into the open sea. There it was dangerous enough, but not to be compared with the deadly trap of Apia Harbour – the trap in which the wild Pacific held its victims and remorselessly destroyed them.

We drove into the hurricane – drove blindly, because it was impossible to see either ahead or around us. We might, for anything we could tell, have been going directly on to some part or other of the reefs skirting the harbour; but we had to risk that, and on we went, smothered in the turmoil, deafened and confused by it all.

Suddenly the *Trenton,* which was the American flagship, loomed up out of the tumult – straight in the fairway, directly in our path, and that path so small, so perilous! It was terrible to see her, more terrible, if that were possible, to think of our own extremity and lessened chance of escape. She was an old cruiser of 4000 tons and the biggest ship in harbour. But by that time she was a floating hulk, hopelessly crippled, with her fires drowned, and clinging to her last and only hope of safety – her cables.

It was afternoon when we passed her, so dangerously close that our yards actually went under hers as we rolled. Her brave old admiral – Kimberley, he is dead now – was on the bridge, and as we fought our way past her we heard a cheer that rose even above the uproar of the storm.

A cheer at such a time! And why? Because, as he said afterwards, "it was a gallant thing," and our captain did it so well that it could not have been done better, and "because," he added, "blood *is* thicker than water." The admiral led the cheers himself, and we responded with a hoarseness that was not altogether due to the weather, bad as it was. Then we were hidden in the whirl of the spindrift, still driving blindly towards salvation, the only ship that would or could make an effort to reach the open water.

Now, I think you will understand what the motion of the *Calliope* was like when we were really punching into it. You may understand I say. I hope so, because no words of mine can make you realise fully what actually happened. Those heavy warships were picked up and thrown about like chips by the savage seas, and the people on board were hurled about as furiously. There was no standing, no sitting, no lying down, unless you were clutching something.

One man, I remember, was thrown against the wheel, and had his teeth smashed; another, a carpenter, was torn off his feet, and as he landed back on deck he was hooked by the jaw on to some projection, and so badly mauled that he had to be invalided out of the Service. As for me, by some means that I cannot explain, I was gripped by the foot by a wire hawser which took a turn round my ankle, and I only got clear by cutting the rope with an axe. I was shuttle-cocked here and there, battered and bruised in a way that seemed incredible and is indescribable. But we were infinitely better off than the poor fellows in the other ships of whom many were carried overboard bodily, or killed or crippled by the heavy seas.

You ask to what angle the *Calliope* rolled, and how much she pitched? Well, I cannot tell, but I suppose that according to all theorists she ought to have rolled over and pitched the vitals out of her as she fell head over heels or stern over stem. But she did none of these things; she plugged at it, through that awful hurricane and those tremendous seas which came from all quarters at once and raised a very whirlpool. How amazingly she had been buffeted I knew from my own body at the finish of the fight. I was completely black with bruises; so much so, that when I went to the doctor I said: "Do you want to see a nigger, sir?" And he thought he saw one, too, when I

We passed her so dangerously close, that our yards actually went under hers as we rolled.

unshipped a towel which was the only thing I was wearing just then as clothing. And I was merely typical of the rest of the ship's company. There was no officer or man who had not his bark or bruise or worse to show as a memento of his thrashing. When you remember what the seas were like, and how the wrecked ships were treated, you can only marvel more and more that the *Calliope* got clear of the harbour as she did, and that she saved herself.

Shall I tell you why I think she survived? Because she was British built, British manned. That sounds boastful, maybe; but I do not mean it to be so. It is only the bare and sober truth. Nothing but the finest and most honest workmanship could bear the punishment of the Pacific hurricane. We had both. Nothing but the best of British officers could have pulled us through. We had them also. And the engineers and stokers! Who can say enough of what they did, and what they had done, to have machinery so faultless!

I can see now, as vividly as we all saw then, the oilskinned-figure of our captain, as he clung to his place on the bridge. He was there at the beginning, he was there through it all, he was there at the very end. The seas smashed and smothered the cruiser. When the fog of the spume had vanished, when the solid green water had roared back into the sea from which it had been torn, he was there, soaking, battered, wearied, but undaunted still.

From first to last he gripped the bridgerail, looking courageously ahead into the smother and turmoil of it all; from beginning to end he never flinched; and because of his example never a man of the ship's company flinched or weakened either. And I want to say to you, here and now, that in all my forty years at sea, I never knew a British Naval officer who in the hour of peril was not equal to the danger. I never knew one who did not meet with a stiff upper lip. If there was a change at all compared with calmer, safer times you only knew it because, perhaps, his language strengthened like the weather. But, after all, that is the way of the sea; and you must allow something for the weather and sailors, mustn't you?

My story of the *Calliope* is finished when I tell you that we got into the open sea and safety, with three anchors and three boats lost, and other damage done. For more than ten hours the engines had been thrashing her out, with never a flaw revealed in them. Wonderful performance! But then, if there had been a flaw of any sort, the ship would not have lived. She would have shared the fate of the rest; for when we returned to Apia on the 19th there was not a ship afloat. Four of the seven men-of-war had been totally lost; two were stranded, and 130 officers and men were dead.

But of the *Calliope's* entire company not a soul was missing.

* * * * *

I am going to take you to a scene as different from the hurricane at Samoa as anything can be. I will take you from the tiny coral harbour and its roaring fatal seas to the placid waters of the Mediterranean; from the leaping, straining, tearing cruiser in her sea-welter, to a battleship that rides with rocklike steadiness on smooth blue water, from a danger which all men saw and knew to one which the keenest wit of man could not foresee, and that is to H.M.S. *Victoria,* the finest ship of her day, the admiration and envy of the whole world of sailors who knew what a fighting machine was and ought to be.

It was a perfect afternoon, on Thursday, June 22, 1893, and in a region where glorious weather is seen at its best – the coast of Tripoli. The last thing in the world that occurred to anybody was the idea of danger. Yet, in ten minutes, owing to an error of judgement on the part of our Commander-in-Chief while manoeuvring, the *Victoria,* his flagship, had been rammed by the *Camperdown,* and had sunk, bottom upward, in nearly 500 feet of water, taking with her twenty-two officers and 350 men.

I am not going into technicalities – you do not want them – nor into details of the great disaster – those who wish for them can find them in the records of the court-martial and elsewhere; and I am not going to enter into any criticism of anybody. That is not my business. But I am going to say here, at the beginning, that some stories have been told about our gallant Commander-in-Chief, Sir George Tyron, which are only exceeded in their folly by their cruelty. He made a mistake, as all the world knows, by ordering the impossible, and he atoned for it like a brave man by sinking with his ship.

I was in my cabin, thinking of nothing more serious than tea. Tea was ready almost at once, and I crossed to the other side of the ship to take some. The squadron was then nearing the place where we were going to anchor, and all was going well.

Without the slightest warning there was a terrific thud, and for the moment I thought the *Victoria* had struck on a rock.

I heard a sound like that which is made by the running of the bower-cable – just as if the anchor had been let go. As a matter of fact, I found the anchor safe in its place; but I still feel certain that the cable went through the bottom of the ship somewhere. It would touch the bottom of the sea at about seventy fathoms – more than 400 feet – and probably catch in something by making a bight, as we call it, or a loop. So you see, with both ends of the huge cable fast to the ship, if the bight caught hold of anything at the bottom of the sea, the sudden bring-up, or check, would sink any ship in our position. Let me make this point clear to shore people by saying that it would be like driving a pony and trap with the reins dragging. All at once the reins catch a stump, and down goes the pony, over goes the trap – and there you are. That may have happened to the *Victoria,* for all I know.

My place as boatswain was on the forecastle, and I rushed there instantly. A second was enough to make me understand what had happened. The *Camperdown* had rammed us, her stem striking our starboard bow, about twenty feet before the turret, and crushing into us almost to our centre line.

It was bad, terrible; but no one anticipated that the disaster would be so dramatic, so overwhelming, and above all things, so sudden as it really was. There was commotion and excitement, but no panic whatever. The colossal ships parted, and the place that had been filled in the stem of the *Camperdown* admitted a perfect flood of water.

At such a crisis the first thing to be done is to get out what are called collision-mats, the object of which is to try to keep the water out. The mats were lowered over the side, and hung over the huge rent, but you might as well have put sheets of paper there, for water was coming in by the ton.

Even when it was recognised that the damage was so serious everybody kept cool and good-tempered, and thought of nothing but saving the ship. Yet we were on the very threshold of one of the swiftest naval catastrophes on record. It is perfectly certain that not a soul on board believed the end to be so near, or, indeed, imagined that the *Victoria* was doomed. So confident was the Admiral himself that the ship would be saved, that when he saw the boats of the *Dreadnought* being lowered to come to our help, he signalled that they should not be sent – only kept in readiness.

While I was seeing to my duties on the forecastle, the captain and other officers were moving swiftly about, on deck and below, to secure the safety of the ship, and, so that nothing should be left undone, the prisoners were released from the guard-room and the sick taken on deck. All, indeed, who were not wanted below, were ordered on deck, but there were large numbers of engineers and stokers at work – every man at his post.

It is hard for most people to understand what courage and discipline are necessary to make it possible for men who are cooped up below at such a time to hold fast to their duty. On deck there is just a chance of salvation; but away down, far below the water-line, literally imprisoned within steel walls, the hope is slight indeed. So vast and complicated, in fact, is the interior of a modern battleship that you may easily lose your chance of escape simply because you cannot find your way out to the open air. I had been in the *Victoria* two or three months, and yet so little was I acquainted with her interior that, believe me, if I had been below when she foundered I should inevitably have gone down with her, because I should not have known which way to turn to escape.

The first time the peril of our position struck me was when I saw that the *Victoria* listed suddenly and heavily to starboard – that is to say, she was leaning dangerously over on her right side. I exclaimed, "Lord! If I were the Admiral I'd pipe all hands to bathe! That would get us clear of the ship, and give us a chance if she goes!" As soon as I had said this I saw the futility of even such an order, because the *Victoria* was level with the sea forward, buried in the water, which was washing up to the turret.

The turret was a circular mass of steel, containing two guns, each a 110-ton weapon, and very famous in their day. The total weight of guns and turret was more than a thousand tons. As you know, a turret revolves with the guns, which it completely shelters, while a barbette carries the guns on the top, only the guns revolving. You can understand precisely what the *Victoria* looked like when you see the *Sans Parcil,* her sister ship – and a fine ship still. Just behind the turret were the conning-tower and the forebridge, above the forebridge was the chart-house, and the roof of the chart-house was what we called the monkey-bridge. Really it was the Admiral's bridge, the spot from which he directed the movements of the fleet.

Sir George Tyron was a stout, heavy man, and generally sat in a chair on his little bridge. But he was standing now, having hurried to his place from the stern-walk, where he had been laughing and joking a minute before the collision. He and Staff-Commander Hawkins Smith, who died not long ago, were together and the Admiral from that high position had a perfectly clear and unimpeded view of the awful havoc which had arisen from his strange mistake. I wonder if anyone has ever realised what his sensations were during those few minutes which passed between the ramming and the sinking of the flagship?

The forecastle was like a cataract by his time, and I was knee-deep in water. I looked up towards the monkey-bridge, and saw that the Admiral wanted me. He called out to me to go and see that the foremost hatch was properly closed down. I never saw him again – and I believe that those were the last words he spoke. He had his hands on the rail, and never moved.

I struggled through the water as well as I could and got to the hatch. Then I knew that all was over, for the water which was filling the ship was bursting through the hatch. This meant, if it meant anything, that there was such a vast quantity of water flooding the ship that she would never get free of it.

It was now every man for himself. I dashed past the turret to the port side, which was high out of the sea, and met the gunner. He exclaimed: "Oh, Bill! What's up?"

I answered: "It's all right. We shall swim like thieves in a minute!"

I never saw him again. Almost instantly I ran up against Lieutenant Munro, and exchanged a few words with him. He hurried into the centre battery – and that was the last I saw of him also. He was amongst the drowned. Those are little instances of the short meetings and long partings which took place when the *Victoria* was lost.

I am now coming to the most terrible part of my story – a part which I would fain pass over and forget for ever. But such a happening cannot be removed from your mind. It is tattooed on your memory.

With the same suddeness as she had been struck, the battleship heeled over – a long, resistless, sickening roll on her wounded side, over and over until her decks were vertical, and her funnels, one after the other – she had a pair, abreast – were in the sea. Then she capsized absolutely, shot head first into the blue waters of the Mediterranean, and with a sound of escaping steam, an explosion of the compressed air within her, and a mad whirring in the air of her twin screws, she disappeared. Just as she went over, her massive turret, with the two huge guns, broke adrift.

That I saw with my own eyes, and I have little doubt that the breaking loose of such an enormous weight had something to do with the final heel.

The battleship, I say, went down, and I went down with her. Swarms of men who had been drawn up on deck jumped into the sea. Some got clear of the vortex, and were rescued by the boats; some were carried down and never rose; some were caught on the blades of the propeller and cut to pieces.

I was standing by one of the anchor cables when she plunged, and I sank with the ship. Death seemed certain; yet, even then, I did not abandon hope, I saw just one slender chance of salvation, and that was to cling to the chain as long as possible until I got clear of the vortex and suction at the surface, then to let go suddenly, give myself a twist to get as free of the sinking ship as I could, and trust to luck to shoot upward. Once afloat, I knew that my safety would be pretty well assured, because by this time boats were swarming on the water. I had this great thing in my favour – I kept cool. I kicked off one of my shoes – they were a black pair – almost, I imagine, the only pair of that colour on board, because it was in the Mediterranean custom to wear white canvas shoes. But the other shoe was too tight to be kicked off, and I kept it on. Here it is – I have painted and decorated it, you see, and keep it as a relic and an ornament.

No one can realise what it meant to keep to that resolve to go down to the last extremity before letting go. There was the first dreadful plunge below the surface, then the swift sinking, the sudden change from light to glowing gloom, from the glorious air to suffocation; the increasing pressure of the water, with the roaring in the ears, and as it seemed, the bursting of the brain.

At such a time seconds seem like hours – if, indeed, you can measure mental agony by time. It is hideous enough when you are sinking voluntarily – what, then, of a time like that, with men dead and dying, by the hundred all about you, clinging to a vast steel tomb, with the shock upon you of a catastrophe the like of which had never been known, and all the more numbing because it was so unexpected?

I kept repeating to myself, "Let go and turn right," "Let go and turn right," "Let go and turn right," and in those few moments I had the strange expression burnt into my brain. I was a mere atom on the side of that colossal hull, a fly, as it might be, which is sticking to a block of metal that is sinking; and the proportion of strength was about the same, the chance of getting free and rising just as slight.

Not till all was deeply green and dark about me did I repeat my words for the last time; then, with the courage of despair and the energy of desperation, I released my hold. I let go and turned right, and made a furious bid for the surface. Lucky for me that I was a good swimmer, luckier still that I had trained my powers of endurance as a diver, and could keep below the water longer than most men.

I shot up swiftly, but it seemed as if I should never reach the top, never get the air again into my panting lungs. Any diver will understand; and those who do not dive or swim can know the sensation by plunging the head into a bath or basin and keeping it there, submerged, until they must either breathe or burst.

But the darkness gave place to growing light, there was a swift transition from oppression and gloom to freedom and sunshine. Never, I think, was liberty so sweet, never air so welcome, so life-renewing! As soon as I bobbed up, one of the *Dreadnought's* boats made for me. The water was dotted with boats from the neighbouring ships, and their crews were grabbing at the struggling survivors, those who had been fortunate enough to be on deck when the *Victoria* went over, and who, like myself, had kept clear of the screws and the vortex.

I was clutched by friendly hands, and was being hauled into the boat. Who can describe my feelings of joy and gratitude? Then an astonishing thing happened. I was let go – and why? Because somebody in the boat shouted: "Hullo! there's Lord ----," mentioning a certain noble lord who was an officer in the *Victoria*, and who was floating about like the rest of us.

A lord is a lord all the world over, at all times – and they went for him and then came back for me. Exhausted though I was, I could not help begging them not to trouble about me till they were quite satisfied that there were no more noble lords afloat or awash, assuring them that as I had waited so long, an extra spell could not make any difference. But they did not waste words on me – they hauled me into the boat, and I collapsed. I realised at once how vain my sarcasm was, for I was so utterly done up that

As soon as I bobbed up, one of the *Dreadnought's* boats made for me.

if I had been put back into the water I should have sunk like a stone and made no effort to save myself.

I was taken on board the *Dreadnought,* and found – so small is the world and so strange the meetings and coincidences of life – that the doctor who took charge of me was the doctor to whom I had presented myself as a nigger in the *Calliope.*

I was exhausted, stunned with the swiftness and magnitude of the disaster – but with vitality enough left to picture the descent to the dark sea-bed of that vast steel tomb in which, at any rate, the prisoners had found a mercifully speedy death.

Less than a quarter of an hour before, the proudest flagship in the world, representing a million pounds sterling, had been floating in security on a calm blue sea in brilliant sunshine, with the laugh and joke going round, a mass of strength, a home of life – and now she was still and buried in the darkness of the sea-bed nearly five hundred feet below us.

And the place where she had floated and made her last appalling dive was marked by struggling sailors and a torn, white sea.

LOCAL HEROES

JAMES W. BANCROFT

THE HOUSE OF HEROES LIBRARY

LOCAL HEROES (Limited Edition)

ISBN: 1-872619-03-7   Price: £4.95p   64pp   210 mm x 150 mm

An illustrated chronicle of sixteen incidents for which the George Cross, Britain's highest civilian gallantry medal has been awarded. Stories of great bravery include an RAF officer who climbed into a blazing aircraft in an attempt to rescue two trapped pilots; the steel nerve displayed by bomb disposal personnel during the Blitz; and two police officers who received serious gunshot wounds as they tried to apprehend dangerous criminals. Many acts of unselfish gallantry were performed in factories, mines and on the railway; including the heroism of a worker who entered a vat of scalding steam to try to save the lives of two teenagers. The author has discovered much information new to the annals of the George Cross.

THE ZULU WAR VCs (Limited Edition)

ISBN: 1-872619-01-0   Price: £19.95p   144pp   260 mm x 180 mm

A collection of extensive biographical tributes, bringing the twenty-three men who gained the Victoria Cross for the Zulu War together in one independent volume. It provides re-examined, detailed narratives of major incidents in the campaign, based on first-hand accounts. The author gives a background to each man, follows his military career, and tells what happened to them in later life. The text is complemented with carefully chosen engravings, photographs and colour-plates. Full colour cover.

'THE BRAVEST DEED' (Limited Edition)

Price: £9.95p   290 mm x 195 mm

A superb action colour-print by the late Richard Scollins depicting Lieutenant Henry Lysons and Private Edmund Fowler, 90th Light Infantry, gaining the Victoria Cross during the desperate fighting at Hlobane Mountain, Zulu War, 1879. Colonel Evelyn Wood VC, said it was 'The bravest deed I ever saw performed in my life.'

THE ZULU WAR VCs

JAMES W. BANCROFT